THE POLITICS OF DEFENCE BUDGETING

RUSI DEFENCE STUDIES SERIES

General Editor David Bolton, Director, Royal United Services Institute for Defence Studies

Editor Jennifer Shaw, MA, BSc(Econ)

Questions on defence give rise to emotion, sometimes to the detriment of balanced judgement. Since 1831 the Royal United Services Institute for Defence Studies has been noted for its objectivity, independence and initiative; the views of its members sharpened by responsibility and experience. In continuance of the Institute's aims, the *RUSI Defence Studies Series* seeks to provide a wider understanding and better informed debate of defence and national security issues. However, the views expressed in the books are those of the authors alone.

Published

Christopher Coker
US MILITARY POWER IN THE 1980s

Christopher Coker
THE FUTURE OF THE ATLANTIC ALLIANCE

Michael D. Hobkirk
THE POLITICS OF DEFENCE BUDGETING

Forthcoming

Christopher Coker
NATO, THE WARSAW PACT AND AFRICA

David Greenwood
BRITISH DEFENCE PRIORITIES

Michael Leifer (editor)
THE ASIAN BALANCE OF POWER

Clive Rose
CAMPAIGNS AGAINST WESTERN DEFENCE: NATO's ADVERSARIES AND CRITICS

THE POLITICS OF DEFENCE BUDGETING

A Study of Organisation and Resource Allocation in the United Kingdom and the United States

Michael D. Hobkirk

formerly Senior Research Fellow
National Defense University, Washington, D.C.

Foreword by
Vice Admiral M. Staser Holcomb

MACMILLAN

Opinions, conclusions, and recommendations expressed or implied within are solely those of the author, and do not necessarily represent the views of the National Defense University, the US Department of Defense, or the UK Ministry of Defence or any other government agency in either the United Kingdom of Great Britain and Northern Ireland or the United States of America.

First published by National Defense University Press 1983
First published by Macmillan 1984

Published by
THE MACMILLAN PRESS LTD
London and Basingstoke
Companies and representatives throughout the world

Printed and bound in Great Britain at
The Camelot Press Ltd, Southampton

British Library Cataloguing in Publication Data
Hobkirk, Michael D.
The politics of defence budgeting.
1. Great Britain—Armed Forces—
Appropriations and expenditures 2. United
States—Armed Forces—Appropriations and
expenditures
I. Title
355.6'22'0941 UA649
ISBN 0-333-38349-4

Contents

Figures and Tables

FIGURES

TABLES

Acronyms

ABM	Anti-Ballistic Missile
ACDS(Ops)	Assistant Chief of the Defence Staff (Operations) (UK)
ACDS(Pol)	Assistant Chief of the Defence Staff (Policy) (UK)
ACDS(S)	Assistant Chief of the Defence Staff (Signals) (UK)
ACSA(N)	Assistant Chief Scientific Adviser Nuclear (UK)
AF	Armed Forces (UK and US)
AG	Adjutant General (UK and US)
AMP	Air Member for Personnel (UK)
AMSO	Air Member for Supply and Organisation (UK)
CA	Controller, Aircraft (UK)
CAS	Chief of the Air Staff (UK)
CBO	Congressional Budget Office (US)
CDP	Chief of Defence Procurement (UK)
CDS	Chief of the Defence Staff (UK)
CER	Controller of Research and Development Establishments and Research (UK)
CFS	Chief of Fleet Support
CGS	Chief of the General Staff (UK)
CNP	Chief of Naval Personnel and Second Sea Lord (UK)
CNS	Chief of Naval Staff and First Sea Lord (UK)
CofN	Controller of the Navy (UK)
CPR	Chief of Public Relations (UK)
CSA	Chief Scientific Adviser (UK)
DCDP(N)	Deputy Chief of Defence Procurement (Nuclear) (UK)
DCDP(P)	Deputy Chief of Defence Procurement (Policy) (UK)
DCDS(OR)	Deputy Chief of the Defence Staff (Operational Requirements) (UK)
DCSA(P)	Deputy Chief Scientific Adviser (Projects) (UK)
DEPC	Defence Equipment Policy Committee (UK)
DGI	Director-General of Intelligence (UK)
DOAE	Defence Operational Analysis Establishment (UK)
DOD	Department of Defense (US)
DP	Defence Procurement (UK)
DPM	Draft Presidential Memorandum (US)
DPRC	Defense Program Review Committee (US)
DUS	Deputy Under-Secretary of State (UK)
DUS(FB)	Deputy Under-Secretary of State (Finance and Budget)

DUS(CM)	Deputy Under-Secretary of State (Civilian Management) (UK)
DUS(P)	Deputy Under-Secretary of State (Policy) (UK)
DUS(PL)	Deputy Under-Secretary of State (Personnel and Logistics) (UK)
DUS(Pol)(PE)	Deputy Under-Secretary of State (Policy) (Procurement Executive) (UK)
HDS	Head of Defence Sales (UK)
ICBM	InterContinental Ballistic Missile
IRBM	Intermediate-Range Ballistic Missile
JCS	Joint Chiefs of Staff (US)
JSOP	Joint Strategic Objectives Plan (US)
MGO	Master-General of the Ordnance (UK)
MOD	Ministry of Defence (UK)
NSC	National Security Council (US)
NOA	New Obligational Authority (US)
OKW	Oberkommando der Wehrmacht
OMB	Office of Management and Budget (US)
OR	Operational Research *or* Operational Requirement
ORC	Operational Requirements Committee (UK)
OSA	Office of Systems Analysis (US)
OSD	Office of Secretary of Defense (US)
PA&E	Program Analysis and Evaluation, Office of (formerly the Office of Systems Analysis) (US)
PCP	Program Change Proposal (US)
PESC	Public Expenditure Survey Committee (UK)
PPBS	Planning, Programming, and Budgeting System (US)
PUS	Permanent Under-Secretary of State (often abbreviated to Permanent Secretary) (UK)
QMG	Quartermaster General (UK)
RAF	Royal Air Force
SA	Systems Analysis (US)
SLBM	Submarine-Launched Ballistic Missile
SofS	Secretary of State for Defence (UK)
USAF	United States Air Force
USofS(AF)	Parliamentary Under-Secretary of State for Defence (Armed Forces) (UK)
USofS(DP)	Parliamentary Under-Secretary of State for Defence (Defence Procurement) (UK)
VCAS	Vice Chief of the Air Staff (UK)
VCDS(P&L)	Vice Chief of the Defence Staff (Personnel and Logistics) (UK)
VCGS	Vice Chief of the General Staff (UK)
VCNS	Vice Chief of the Naval Staff (UK)

Preface

David Bolton

Resource allocation and the proper management of those resources are central themes in the defence debate. That debate will intensify through the decade of the 1980s. The RUSI Defence Studies Series, with the publication of this book, seeks to provide a better understanding of the issues involved. The author, Michael Hobkirk, with his considerable Whitehall experience and his Visiting Senior Research Fellowship at the National Defense University in Washington, is ideally suited to the task.

In the United States, the Reagan Administration has resolutely sought to redress the period of a stagnating defence economy throughout the 1970s with large injections of money. It is questionable if such expenditure can be sustained; already there is evidence of it being curtailed. There is also talk of the mismanagement of defence funds. In Europe, the record of NATO member nations in meeting the 1977 agreed policy of a real annual increase of 3 per cent in defence expenditure is patchy at best. The prospect of acceding to SACEUR's request for a 4 per cent annual real increase would therefore seem remote.

In the United Kingdom, the decision has been taken not to maintain the 3 per cent annual increase in defence expenditure after 1985–6. Yet the UK is committed to a national strategic nuclear deterrent, the defence of the UK base, and maintaining its contribution both to the NATO forces in Europe and the Atlantic command of the Alliance. This takes scarce account of the costs of maintaining forces to secure the Falkland Islands, or of developing and procuring weapon systems which take advantage of emerging technology.

Admiral of the Fleet, The Lord Lewin, GCB, MVO, DSC, was instrumental in 1982 in a reorganisation of the UK Ministry of Defence which gave greater power and a stronger central staff to the Chief of Defence Staff in order to produce a more cohesive defence policy. Now, in 1984, The Secretary of State for Defence, Michael Heseltine, has taken a much more radical view and proposed a 'clearer distinction between:

(a) the formulation of advice on operations, defence policy, and resource allocation—which are central to the Ministry; and
(b) the management of the Services themselves which I have already

> said I wish to see decentralised as far as practicable outside MOD, progressively under a regime of responsibility budgets.'

The Defence Staff would be charged with 'the corporate duty of finding the best defence solution to the problems of the day, whether of an operational nature, strategic planning, defence policy or equipment priorities'. The management of each service, through executive committees, would be the principle concern of the Service Chiefs of Staff, denied their own policy staffs which, it is proposed, should be hived-off to a fully unified and integrated military/civilian defence policy and operations staff. Responsibility for finance and budget, resource allocation and audit would be concentrated in a new Office of Management and Budget (OMB) with its own Controller-General. A streamlining in scientific research and development is also recommended. However, the field of defence equipment procurement is still under separate examination. Details of the proposal are included as an annex to this book.

The proposed reorganisation is designed to produce a simpler and more efficient structure. It remains to be seen how effective such a radical restructuring will be. That it resembles the hypothetical ideal of Michael Hobkirk serves to illustrate his prescience. In any event, an examination of the underlying issues from an historical perspective, can only serve to provide a clearer view of the arguments and a more balanced judgment on the outcome in an era of changing strategic requirements funded from more constrained resources.

Foreword

By Vice Admiral M. Staser Holcomb, US Navy
Deputy Commander-in-Chief, United States Naval Forces Europe

Michael Hobkirk's comparative study of the defence budgeting processes which operate in the United Kingdom and the United States is both timely and discerning. Timely, because significant changes in the processes are now under consideration in both countries, as this volume goes to press. In mid-March 1984, UK Secretary of State for Defence Michael Heseltine made a surprise announcement of his reorganisation plan for the Ministry of Defence, a plan bolder than any reform attempted in the 20-year history of the Ministry. Meanwhile, hearings within the US Congress over the past year appear to have set the stage for new legislation with respect to the organisation of the Joint Chiefs of Staff and the role of the Armed Services in resource allocation. Discerning, because the study reviews how the defence organisations in the two countries have evolved since the end of the Second World War, who the players are—civilian and uniformed—in each system, and what might be done to better the decision-making processes. Starting with the advantage of a clean slate, Michael Hobkirk develops the model organisation for a fictional European nation, Ruritania. What he comes up with is remarkably similar to the thrust of the Heseltine proposals. It also has a parallel in what reformists propose in the United States. Details of the Heseltine proposals are included as an Annex to this book.

As a serving US naval officer, with fairly extensive experience over the past 20 years in the Planning, Programming, and Budgeting System introduced by Robert McNamara in 1961, I found myself on familiar ground throughout Hobkirk's analysis. Nevertheless, his perspective, as a retired career bureaucrat in the UK system, is bound to differ from my own. Inter-Service rivalry—fierce budgetary competition between strong, independent armed services—may be the villain in the piece; a powerful central policy and planning staff could emerge as a saviour. But things are frequently not as simple as that, although such themes can be heard in the US, particularly among reformists.

Of course, there is inertia in any large organisation, along with an unquestionable instinct for survival. In the United States, the Army (780 000 strong), the Navy (560 000), the Air Force (600 000), and the Marine Corps (165 000) are large institutions. That said, the military tasks assigned to each under a unified command scheme, which deals with joint defence on a global scale, call for force structure and weapons systems well beyond what any of the Services could expect to attain independently. This is reflected in often-disparaged recommendations of the Joint Chiefs of Staff, who, charged with reviewing each year the forces and deployments necessary to reduce the risk of being unable to carry out the agreed strategy, have consistently asked for more of everything than the individual Services requested. So a great deal more than inter-Service rivalry is at play in formulating US defence budgets.

There are fundamental differences between the ways our two countries go about the business of government and, hence, defence. Hobkirk explores these carefully. Even so, more weight might properly be given to the role of Congress in decision-making relative to US defence. Specifically empowered by the Constitution to 'raise and support Armies' and to 'provide and maintain a Navy', the Congress jealously guards its prerogatives with respect to every aspect of the Armed Services. The operative principle is: the Executive proposes, the Congress disposes.

The Congressional disposition process disintegrates the Executive's budget proposals and enacts appropriations in a traditional fashion. In the Armed Services Committees, authorisation of R & D, procurements and manpower take place, Service by Service, on a line-item basis. In a way not precisely overlapping the authorisation recommended by the desired Services Committee, pay, procurements and operations are treated line-item by line-item by both House and Senate Appropriations Committees. Intelligence is sliced off by yet other committees; and so on. Only in the work of the Budget Committees in both Houses, active since the late 1970s, is the 'defence function' addressed in the aggregate; even there, it is in terms of input—a budget ceiling—rather than function, mission or output. Moreover, the appropriations process, which is the object of the game, has a two-year horizon at best, because that is the life of a Congress, so it tends to reflect constituencies and special interests in the Congress rather than any overall national strategy.

Confronting Congress with centrally-developed, tightly rationalised budget proposals in the early 1960s, Secretary McNamara seized the initiative—for a while. But by the end of the decade, Congressional staffs had swelled with analysts, econometricians, and program appraisers, many of whom had gained experience in the Executive Branch. Both the scope and duration of budget review increased, and the initiative began to swing back toward the legislative branch. There is no parallel for this propose-and-dispose interaction in the UK system.

In essence, US defence budgeting can be characterised as an

adversary process throughout. At the level of any of the individual Services, competition is intense between the various military arms and supporting programs; the product is a compromise between force structure, modernisation, readiness, and long-term sustainability—all within program and fiscal guidance dictated by the Secretary of Defense. Individual weapons systems and projects will have undergone continuous wire-brushing within the whole of the Defense acquisition process before appearing as a line-item in a Service budget. At the next level, the individual Services advocate hard-fought compromise packages with the staff of the Secretary of Defense and Defense Resources Board. The resulting DOD budget proposal, now a matter of advocacy on the part of the Secretary of Defense, must be defended within the frame of reference imposed by the Office of Management and Budget, to become part of the President's Budget. Once that multi-volume document is delivered to Congress, the Executive Branch spends most of the next eight months explaining, justifying, and defending its resource allocations in hearing after hearing. (As director of Navy programme planning and budgeting in 1979–81, I found that various pieces of the Navy's budget had to be managed through no fewer than ten Committees and two dozen sub-committees in both Houses.)

Enormous numbers of professional man-years go into this process every year, essentially reviewing the entire defence programme from a zero base and rejustifying every item. The process can hardly be characterised as efficient, or even coherent. But, being adversarial, it does tend to discard bad ideas, or those which enjoy only narrow support, and it does generate a kind of consensus. It typifies the 'checks and balances' which were considered to be so important by the nation's founding fathers two centuries ago. Because there are few aspects of the national defence decision-making problem for which precise, point solutions can be defined, that may be more a virtue than a fault.

In contrast to the way things have come to work in US defence decision-making, Michael Hobkirk argues for a powerful central policy, planning and budgeting staff. He also argues for a budgeting system with functional categories or programmes directly related to the specific tasks of the armed forces, a long-term or multi-year system which provides as stable an environment as possible for future plans. Those are ends devoutly to be desired. They may be attainable in Ruritania, but they appear unlikely to take hold in the US adversarial framework. It remains to be seen whether the Heseltine proposals are likely to bring them to effect in the UK.

May 1984

Note on Spelling

This study contains a large number of words that are spelled differently in Britain and the United States. English (as opposed to American) spelling has been used throughout, except in quotations from American authors; in the titles of US government posts (e.g. Secretary of Defense), and for words (such as 'program') which have a special meaning in US defence business.

Chapter One

Is This Book Necessary?

Strategy, programs, and budget are all aspects of the same basic decisions.

Harry S. Truman[1]

As the road to hell is paved with good intentions, so the path to defence organisation is well carpeted with good advice. The wise men tell us that advice, good or bad, is never welcome, so the writer who is rash enough to add to the existing pile of books on this subject in the United States and, to a lesser extent in the United Kingdom, must have a good excuse. This book offers two.

First, it does not look as if the defence organisations in the United Kingdom or the United States are yet quite right. They have not yet organised themselves so as to avoid defence policy being a compromise between the conflicting views of the three Armed Services.[2] It is true that in 1982 the British Secretary of State for Defence announced that the authority of the Chief of the Defence Staff (his senior, Service adviser) was to be enhanced so that he became just that, rather than the chairman of a committee of three single-Service Chiefs of Staff required, if at all possible, to reconcile their views before presenting them to the government. (This topic is discussed more fully in chapter 3.) But if this change is the final step in organising the Ministry of Defence, the British would be well advised to await the test of one more radical defence review before saying so.

On the other side of the Atlantic in the same year, 1982, the Chairman of the Joint Chiefs of Staff, General David C. Jones, US Air Force, pointed out in public that he was no more than the chairman of a committee of three Service Chiefs with conflicting views, and that he was without the authority or the staff to offer independent advice to the Secretary of Defense. (This topic is discussed more fully in chapter 4.) General Jones quoted a large number of previous reviews and reports reaching the same conclusion and pressed for changes similar to those implemented in the United Kingdom earlier that year. Many of those previously responsible for US defence policy publicly endorsed his criticisms. These events in both countries took place between eighteen and twenty-five years after the supposed final reorganisations of both defence departments.

There is no doubt that inter-Service rivalry can impair the effectiveness of defence policy. As John Garnett has pointed out, "the history of inter-Service relationships both in Britain and the United States is full of inter-Service clashes in which the national interest seemed to get lost in a more parochial struggle for organisational survival. In Britain, for example, the issue of whether to abandon the aircraft carrier in 1965–66 may be regarded as a struggle between the Navy and the RAF for limited funds."[3] Professor Garnett goes on to mention Paul Hammond's "Super Carriers and B36 Bombers, Appropriations Strategy, and Politics,"[4] which explains how some strategic weapons were bought after World War II, not for strategic reasons but in response to organisational pressures within the Services. More recent examples, such as the partially successful efforts by the Royal Navy to restore the 1981 cuts in the surface fleet and the successful efforts of the US Air Force (and the aircraft manufacturer concerned) to restore the B1 bomber programme, show that pressure from a Service that dissents from defence policy is not a thing of the past.

The serious cause for concern is not that there is argument and disagreement within the defence departments among the Services, but the extent to which strong feelings may warp judgments, distort facts, and lead to a defence policy that does not make the best use of available resources. During the aircraft carrier controversy in Britain in 1965–66, according to Sir Frank Hopkins, one study of the relative merits of the carrier and shore-based aircraft moved "Australia 600 miles to the northwest in order to bring certain targets within the already elastic radius of action of the F-111."[5] Vincent Davis writes that "Air Force officers [in World War II] sometimes seemed incapable of distinguishing between dedication to country and their dedication to proving the validity of their Douhet-Mitchell strategic ideology."[6]

These last two examples of dedication to Service goals are not of recent origin, but the example noted by John Steinbruner in 1974 still exists and will be discussed in more detail in chapter 11.

> The United States ... maintains conventional war capabilities ... for the defense of Europe.... Toward this end the Army maintains infantry tanks and artillery of various kinds. The Air Force for its part operates fighter planes for air superiority, long range interdiction, and close support of ground forces. Both the Army and the Air Force are clearly engaged in procuring the capacity to concentrate conventional fire power on the enemy. However, the size and character of these separate service programs are not considered in relationship to each other when decisions are made about them.[7]

Steinbruner's example of the effects of inter-Service rivalry over the defence budget, based on a congressional Joint Economic Committee report of 1969, would be generally borne out by the recent criticisms of General Jones, already referred to and discussed in detail in chapter 4. It is apparent that each Service guards its own share of the defence budget carefully, and tends, unless it receives strong directions to the contrary from the President or in the United Kingdom the Defence Secretary, to spend funds on those items that each considers important, regardless of overall defence policy and the needs of the other Services. This process has been called suboptimisation.

A major task of any Defence Secretary in any country should be to ensure that the maximum benefit is derived from the resources devoted to defence. If each Service is allowed to spend its share of the budget according to its own judgment, there will probably be waste and duplication as each of them sets aside funds for tasks that are better done by another Service, or that are of doubtful value anyway. It is also possible that the resulting defence strategy may contain serious gaps because one Service has failed to devote sufficient funds to provide the necessary support for another,[8] leading to what is sometimes called a distorted or disjointed defence budget. To the extent that this happens, inter-Service rivalry is the likely cause. A study of this rivalry may suggest methods of avoiding its bad effects.

A second justification for this study is the insight to be gained by comparing the evolution of two defence organisations that had similar origins in the 1940s, but have developed in different ways since then. In 1982 they both faced the problem of coping with inter-Service rivalry over resource allocation. Despite the work done by Richard Burt in 1975 and by Kenneth Waltz in 1968 in the wider field of political institutions,[9] there are some interesting comparisons still to be made between the UK and US methods of allocating defence resources.

Some may argue that the great difference in scale between the US and UK armed forces invalidates any comparisons between the two defence departments. In some fields (for example, weapons procurement and defence industrial problems) comparisons could be misleading. This study concentrates on the special problem of dividing defence budgets among three Armed Services of approximately equal status. Both countries share this problem, and both defence organisations have much in common. A description of the different ways in which each nation goes about this task may well be illuminating.

Comparative studies of defence organisations can fulfill a number of useful purposes. First, to study another's organisation can help one to understand one's own better, by learning which aspects of it are unique and which are shared with similar organisations elsewhere.[10] This understanding is particularly important if certain aspects of organisation, procedure, or techniques are to be borrowed from elsewhere. Another argument in favour of learning more about other defence departments can be found along with much else of value about bureaucratic politics in Richard Neustadt's *Alliance Politics*.[11] That book ends with a plea for greater understanding of the inner politics of allies. Failure to understand allies, he argues, leads to failure to influence them. Finally, there is the hope that comparative studies such as this will provide the basis on which others can build more comprehensive theories of organisation and decisionmaking.

This study starts by tracing in chapters 3 and 4 the evolution of the central organisations for defence in the United Kingdom and the United States. At first they appeared very similar, but over the years they have developed very different structures and methods for managing the resource allocation process. The search for an explanation of these differences will lead outside the defence organisation itself, and it will be found helpful to use Morton Halperin's concept of the "rules of the game" for participation in the decision process.[12] Halperin has pointed out that some rules derive from constitutional and legislative delegation of power. It will become clear that the structure of government in the United States has a decisive influence on their method of defence resource management. By contrast, British traditions of government have shaped a different style of defence management, in which decisions about the allocation of resources are neither debated publicly in advance nor even much discussed outside those government departments concerned with defence, finance, and foreign policy.

Halperin also mentions as part of the rules of the game the unwritten code of ethics determining how each participant relates to others in the bureaucracy. His idea will help to structure the chapters describing both the bureaucracies and their methods of budgeting, financial control, and management. The two countries' different approaches toward the defence budget does much to explain their different styles of defence management.

Chapter 11 looks at the different methods that US and UK defence planners might use to solve a hypothetical, but not unlikely, problem. The final two chapters look at possible solutions to the problem of inter-Service rivalry and suggest some of the essential ingredients of an ideal defence organisation. But the first step is to examine in chapter 2 the relevance of certain theories of organisation and decisionmaking to current problems of defence organisation.

Chapter Two
Can Theory Help?

The previous chapter has established that there is dissatisfaction in the United States and to a lesser extent in the United Kingdom about the ability of the two defence departments, as presently organised, to deal with the problem of inter-Service rivalry. Also mentioned were some of the results of this rivalry in the past. It is now important to establish whether writers on the theory of organisation can account for the apparent unwillingness of the Armed Services to accept subordination of their own goals to those of the defence organisation as a whole. If bureaucratic politics of this type exist elsewhere, then those who write on decision theory may be able to illuminate the process of making decisions about resource allocation and suggest ways of improving the process.

ORGANISATION THEORY

Bureaucracy has been under study, first by Max Weber and then by many others, since the early part of this century. Weber's standard model of bureaucracy still seems valid. His model involves organisation by function, with personnel assigned to specialised tasks, a hierarchy of authority for control and supervision, and the establishment of policy guidance for all activities, with the most important administrative directives being preserved in written form. Bureaucracies are by this definition as common outside government as within. They are in fact the rational, universal institution of large-scale enterprise.[1] The term can, of course, be applied as readily to military as to civilian institutions; indeed the Prussian General Staff as it developed in the middle of the last century has good claims to be considered as the first large-scale modern bureaucracy.

Once it is accepted that the US and UK defence organisations are bureaucracies, possibly in some formulations the largest in their respective countries, then the problem of inter-Service rivalry can be set in the wider context provided by those who have written on the theory of organisation.[2] Of course it must be accepted that Administrative Man, that is the bureaucrat, is an abstraction like Economic Man, but it is a helpful one to use when exploring the inner workings of an organisation. Above all, it must be stressed that Administrative Man is, within the limits imposed by circumstance and the organisation, a rational man. "The ends of organisation," C.I. Barnard writes, "to a relatively high degree involve logical processes not as rationalisations after decision but as processes of decisions. Moreover, when ends have been adopted, coordination of acts as means to these ends is essentially a logical process."[3] Administrative Man therefore seeks to act rationally to achieve the goals of his organisation. Indeed, it is only on the basis of rational action that he can work with others in the organisation to achieve shared objectives. If, then, serious conflicts exist between subunits of an organisation that should be working together, it is reasonable to look first at the structure of the organisation for an explanation.

This proposition becomes plainer if one looks more closely at the process of policymaking in a bureaucracy. "In retrospect at least," according to John Garnett, "policy is revealed by a series of decisions, and in prospect it is revealed by general statements of purpose.... Policy is best thought of not as a series of finite decisions but as a flow of purposive action over a period of time."[4] But, as Raymond Bauer writes, "the intellectual activities of perception, analysis, and choice, often subsumed under the rubric decisionmaking, are carried on within a social context of organisational structures, competing bureaucratic groups, and so forth."[5] If the activities of perception and analysis in any area are conducted exclusively by the subgroup responsible for that area of policy, then those in charge of the whole organisation are likely to be under pressure to consider and decide on the problems of each subgroup separately without surveying the needs and policies of the organisation as a whole. This tendency, called by Cyert and March "sequential attention to goals,"[6] is obviously harmful to any attempt at a coherent policy for the whole organisation. As John Steinbruner writes of this explanation of decisionmaking, "the problem of aggregating across different individuals who are involved in the decision process is solved by avoiding it."[7]

If this phenomenon of sequential attention to goals is relatively common in large-scale organisations, it is perhaps surprising that inter-Service rivalry has attracted particular attention. Part of the explanation must be that defence is big business, and public business, so that some of the harmful results of this rivalry are obvious to the outsider. The underlying reason is surely that war has changed in the last forty years with the result that separate land and sea battles are for the most part a thing of the past. Large-scale combat is now likely to involve two and possibly three of the Services (on each side), and there is no longer a clear distinction of roles between them.

The existence of three Services in separate organisations, with their identities reinforced by their different uniforms, tends to stress the somewhat arbitrary nature of the present distribution of roles and missions among them. How heavy and complex must a combat or a transport aircraft for the land battle be for it to remain an Army responsibility? When Army, or Marine, units are to fight on land after a long sea voyage should the last stage of their journey from ship to beach, either by assault craft or by helicopter, be the responsibility of the Navy, the Army, or the Air Force? These problems of interface can also occur when future weapons and equipment are being planned. Thus one Service may find that equipment or weapons which it deems vital—for example, close-support aircraft or logistic ships—are of less interest to the Service responsible for providing them from a limited budget. On another occasion, one Service may seem to the other two to be preempting too large a share of the defence budget for a particular role or a weapon system, with the result that strategy may, they fear, be dangerously distorted to take account of it.

Some examples of the harmful effects of inter-Service rivalry mentioned in chapter 1 came from an article written by John Garnett with the title "Constraints on Defence Policy Makers." Clearly, he considers this rivalry to be one of the significant constraints, but by no means the only one. If the problems of defence organisation and defence resource allocation are to be set in their proper context, the highly complex nature of large-scale organisations must be appreciated. Harold Leavitt has described such organisations as "lively sets of interrelated systems designed to perform complicated tasks." He goes on to point out that "we can try to manipulate at least three of those systems in order to get the performance of tasks changed or improved.[8] John Dawson has applied the Leavitt management model to "top level decisionmaking regarding American defense resources" as shown in figure 2:1.[9] When the model is applied to the UK defence organisation, some different items would appear in each of the boxes on the diagram, but the diagram itself (and the interactions between the boxes) is still valid.

The model is a valuable reminder that the organisational and procedural changes examined later in this book cannot provide a complete solution to every problem faced by a Defence Secretary. Even if the perfect defence organisation is ever created, it will only delete one of the constraints listed in figure 2.1. When, for instance, a Defence Secretary receives impeccable military advice, he may find himself prevented from acting on it by some item under the heading "People." This constraint could be the strong feelings aroused in the Service adversely affected by the proposal, or the lack of political support (in the United Kingdom, this would be in the cabinet and government party; in the United States the term is more imprecise but would have to include congressional support), or he may

Figure 2.1
US Defence Resource Allocation Decisionmaking

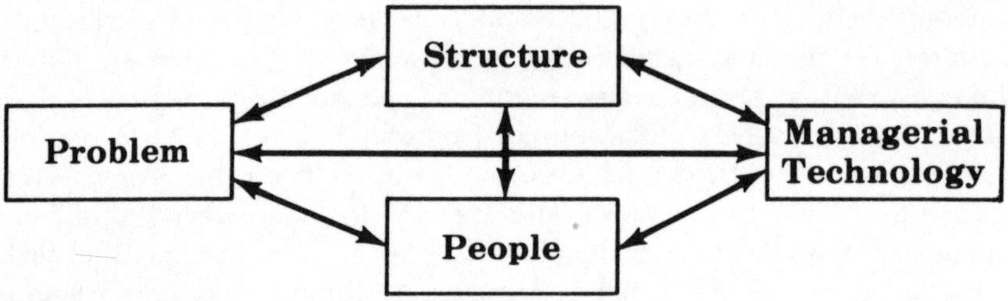

The Problem

(1) Geographical position and international involvement.
(2) Scientific/technological advances in weaponry.
(3) The dimension of distance and the task of logistics.
(4) The dimension of time and its military utility.

Structure

(1) Constitutional-political relationships.
(2) The President as Commander in Chief.
(3) The interface and internal organisation of bureaucracies for military and civilian affairs.
(4) The institutionalisation of effective civilian control.

People

(1) The personalities and proclivities of Presidents, Congressmen and Senators, high political appointees, members of the Joint Chiefs of Staff, and other general officers.
(2) Selective attention (and inattention) given by the preceding to the views of staff personnel, think-tank analysts, reporters and media leaders, and dissenters.
(3) Perceptions among people in both of the preceding categories regarding what the public generally is prepared to do, support, or tolerate.

Managerial Technology

(1) Systems for the design, procurement, support, deployment, and utilisation of men, equipment, and materiel integrated as forces.
(2) Systems analysis, programme budgeting—PPB and all that.

Source: John Dawson, "An American View of Defence Management," in *The Management of Defence*, ed. L. Martin (London: 1976), pp. 48, 49. Reprinted by permission of the author.

find that he has against him a tide of public opinion that may or may not have been translated into active political opposition. Any or all of these factors might justify the Chief Executive (or Defence Secretary) in not acting on the advice offered.

Readers will no doubt identify numerous examples of the working of Leavitt's model in defence, especially in chapters 3 and 4, which trace the history of UK and US defence organisations. Factors in the boxes marked "Structure" and "People" in figure 2.1 provide much of the explanation for the reversal of Mr. Sandys' defence policy after 1958 (see chapter 3). Mr. McNamara's decision (described in chapter 4) to change procedures ("Managerial Technology" in figure 2:1) was, as the model shows, as valid a method of trying to diminish the effects of inter-Service rivalry as the many previous and subsequent attempts to achieve the same result by operating on the box marked "Structure." As this is not a study of management theory, no attempt will be made to explain all changes in the two defence organisations by reference to the model. The main conclusion for this study is that changes in the performance of an organisation can be effected either by manipulating structures or techniques or by changing the attitudes of the people involved. Moreover, since the three categories "Structure," "Techniques," and "People" interact, any change in one may have significant effects on the others and hence on the performance of the organisation as a whole.

Organisation theory then accepts that competing groups can appear in any large organisation but gives no support to those who despair of finding a cure for the worst effects of such internal competition. Indeed, by stressing the interactions between various parts, Leavitt provides ground for hope that any reorganisation which sufficiently emphasizes the importance of the centre rather than the component parts may in due course induce the people in the organisation to elevate loyalty to the whole above loyalty to their own part of it. The model itself provides no clue as to how changes can be made, nor does it provide any measure of the relative strength of the various factors involved. Nevertheless, the thrust of the argument of Leavitt and others is that organisations, composed of rational men, should recognize a responsibility to improve their output, which in the case of a central defence organisation must include sound impartial advice on defence policy.

DECISION THEORY

Even if organisations can be changed to improve output, those who write about decision theory stress the immense complexity of the task of those responsible for public policy. For a start, the problem does not arrive neatly packaged on the decisionmaker's desk. "Most issues," as Graham Allison writes, "emerge piecemeal over time, one lump in one context, a second in another. Hundreds of issues compete for players' attention every day. Each player is forced to fix upon his issues for that day, fight them on his own terms, and rush on to the next."[10]

Moreover, the defence policymaker never starts with a clean sheet on which to design policy. He is constrained by a system of values and by a web of international commitments and domestic pressures that inevitably impose caution in any attempt to change defence policy. In addition, previous decisions about defence will have committed him to force levels and an armoury of weapons either in existence or under construction which cannot be wished away. A step-by-step pragmatic approach is therefore inevitable. Charles Lindblom has described this disjointed or incremental method of problem solving as "the science of muddling through."[11]

Lindblom, however, goes further; he argues that not only is this step-by-step approach, aiming for a satisfactory but not necessarily the best solution to a problem, the way managers (whether in government or a private corporation) actually do solve problems, but that given man's limitations both as a forecaster and as a value-free judge, it is also the most efficient. This description of the step-by-step approach is a convincing explanation of resource allocation (and much else) at the top. How can Presidents or cabinets decide what should be spent for defence and what for nondefence purposes? There is no cost effectiveness analysis to guide them here.

No one is able to measure the relative worth of poor relief and battleships. Only some form of political judgment based on the relative strength of the partisans for defence expenditure on the one hand, and those supporting, for example, increased social expenditure on the other, will produce an answer acceptable to the nation in question. Partisan mutual adjustment[12] can also explain that much disliked habit, which governments have during economy drives, of cutting all areas of public expenditure by roughly the same proportion. This "equal misery" approach has, as Aaron Wildavsky points out,[13] definite advantages because all concerned can view the consequences of a marginal cut in a complex and unpredictable area and then deal with them piecemeal.

Nevertheless, even if total defence expenditure has to accept such arbitrary cuts, is it right to pass them on in equal proportions to the three Services? This approach could imply either that no one could predict with any confidence the effects of deeper cuts on one Service rather than the others, or that the strength of Service feeling was such that the Services were not willing collectively to accept any solution except equal misery for all. These alternatives are not mutually exclusive; perhaps both could apply at once. But if they did, this solution would not inspire confidence.

Even if partisan mutual adjustment correctly describes many government decisions, one might expect a more rational approach within defence itself.

THE ROLE OF ANALYSIS

In more limited situations, such as the comparison of two designs for a new torpedo or two makes of arctic clothing, it seems likely that objective analysis could persuade most of those involved which was the better. Ralph Sanders would classify this method as engineering analysis[14] and suggests the diagram shown in figure 2.2 to chart the fit of analytical techniques to problems:

Figure 2.2
The Fit of Analytical Techniques to Problems

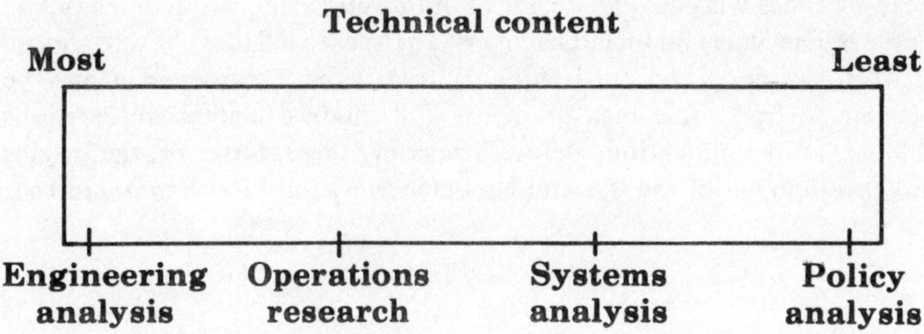

Source: Ralph Sanders, *The Politics of Defense Analysis* (New York: 1973), p. 11. Reprinted by permission of the author.

According to Leavitt, large organisations normally use one of two methods to resolve conflict between competing groups whenever it is important that both should accept the final decision.[15] The first is the "method of measurement," achieving an impersonal decision by using numbers. The second is the "lots of talk solution," involving much discussion and writing over a long period until a decision emerges without anyone being able to identify precisely which individual or body made the final decision. Clearly, in defence resource allocation the "method of measurement" will use operational research and systems analysis; later chapters in this book will argue that these two techniques can play a larger part in resource allocation decisions than they have in the past. Perhaps "lots of talk" would be an unfair description of the way defence policy has been decided in the past, but those who adopt a defence policy that is a compromise between competing pressures from the three Services should at lease consider how far decisions could be improved by resort to the method of measurement.

CONCLUSION

This brief survey of the theories of organisation and decisionmaking has established that bureaucratic politics are not peculiar to defence, and that something similar to inter-Service rivalry may well occur in any large organisation. Nevertheless, any organisation has the duty to improve its product; for a central defence organisation, this duty entails providing advice on a coherent defence policy that is something more than a compromise between the competing demands of the three Services.

Those who write on decision theory are right to stress the difficulties faced by those who have to decide about resource allocation in the public sector.[16] They have no formulae or cost analyses to tell them how to choose between hospitals and battleships. Within defence, however, it may be possible to find some measurements and models to improve decisions about resource allocation. Before discussing these, however, the origins and development of the UK and US defence organisations require further study.

Chapter Three
Central Defence Organisation in the United Kingdom

ORIGINS AND EARLY HISTORY

There has been discussion in the United Kingdom about some form of central defence organisation for over one-hundred years, but until recently the emphasis was on coordination rather than control, with two notable exceptions: Disraeli in 1850[1] and Lord Randolph Churchill in 1890[2] both advocated that one minister should be responsible for the two Armed Services. However, the central defence organisation that evolved from 1904 (when the Committee of Imperial Defence was formed with a permanent secretariat) until 1940 (when Mr. Churchill became Prime Minister and Minister of Defence) was based on committees to coordinate rather than one ministry to control the Services. As Michael Howard says, "during the first half of this century the United Kingdom was defended by interdepartmental committees."[3]

The experience of World War II was studied closely in 1945, but the new defence organisation that came into existence with the creation of a Ministry of Defence in 1946 did not significantly change the position of the Minister of Defence. It is true that the Minister was given general responsibility for apportioning financial resources among the Services. But, as the 1946 White Paper makes clear, the Chiefs of Staff had direct access to the Defence Committee of the cabinet on all questions of strategy and plans, and it was expressly stated that the Minister of Defence would not act as their mouthpiece before the committee. The White Paper further makes the point that it was for the Minister of Defence to bring his proposals on the allocation of resources before the committee. The situation was therefore that the ministers in charge of the Service departments and the Chiefs of Staff had direct access to the Defence Committee, the same body to which the Minister of Defence was invited to submit proposals for sharing available financial resources among the Services. This was clearly evolution and not revolution. Britain was still to be defended by interdepartmental committees.

As Laurence Martin wrote, "to set a crude financial ceiling and leave the selection of strategy and design of forces wholly to bargaining among the Services is frequently regarded as an invitation to aimlessness."[4] Professor Martin describes well the situation in the early fifties in the United Kingdom, and Defence by Bargaining will be used to denote it. The essential feature of this method of resource allocation is the ability of the Service departments to decide on the spending priorities for their shares of the defence budget without any overriding direction from the central defence organisation, save on such major public issues as the ending of compulsory military service or the creation of a nuclear deterrent. Defence policy then becomes a compromise between the competing demands of the three Services.

The period between 1946 and 1957 saw only one significant change in defence organisation—a change that was perhaps less important than it sounded. In October 1955, the post of Chief Staff Officer to the Minister of Defence was converted into that of Chairman of the Chiefs of Staff Committee. But it is important to note that the incumbent was only given a few extra military staff to help him undertake his increased responsibilities.[5] It is hard to see any major results from the creation of this appointment before the arrival of Mr. Duncan Sandys as Minister of Defence in 1957.

THE SANDYS ERA

The appointment of Mr. Sandys in early 1957 led to a considerable extension of the powers of the Minister of Defence. As a result of his own experience as Minister of Defence,[6] Mr. Macmillan as Prime Minister was determined to ensure that defence policy did not fail because of lack of powers for the Minister himself. Therefore, as was announced in the House of Commons in January 1957, the Minister of Defence was granted "authority to give decisions on all matters of policy affecting the size, shape, or organisation and disposition of the armed forces, their equipment and supply (including defence research and development), and their pay and conditions of service."[7] He was also given additional powers on any matters of service administration or appointments that in his view were of importance. This mandate was, it was appreciated, a decisive break with the past. Whereas the 1946 White Paper had emphasised continuity with the past, this brief announcement in the House of Commons produced for the first time a charter for the Minister of Defence, giving him absolute control over resource allocation. It was to be some years yet before this control could be effective in hands other than those of a powerful minister such as Mr. Sandys. Nevertheless, the decisive step away from Defence by Bargaining had been taken.

It was decided not to make any changes in defence organisation until more experience had been gained about the new situation created by the increased powers of the Minister.[8] Nevertheless, 1957, the year in which these powers were first used, was as important for defence organisation in the long-run as 1958, the year in which Mr. Sandys effected the changes in defence organisation that he considered necessary. The 1957 White Paper was claimed to be the most radical change in defence policy ever effected in peacetime, but as Sir John Slessor has pointed out, "a great many of the changes were implicit in decisions which had already been taken both about strategic policy and about weapon procurement."[9] Nevertheless, it was a big step to make the changes explicit and to curtail so many activities that all three of the Services considered vital both for national security and for their own existence in the future. Mr. Sandys spent the months between January and April 1957 in long and heated discussions with the Chiefs of Staff, but the decisions announced in the White Paper were not whole-heartedly accepted by the Chiefs of Staff and the Service ministries.[10] A reallocation of roles and resources among the various Services had been made, and this had implications for defence organisation in the future. Many if not most of the major decisions in the 1957 White Paper (excluding of course the decision about national service) were, in due course, to be reversed or amended; but the effort of securing these changes led inevitably to a new kind of Ministry of Defence, and one which had significant consequences for the 1964 reorganisation.

The changes in organisation announced in the 1958 Defence White Paper added little to the impressive mandate given to the Minister of Defence in 1957. The Minister's responsibilities for a unified defence policy were rephrased but not extended. The Chairman of the Chiefs of Staff Committee was retitled Chief of the Defence Staff (CDS) but given no more powers. A Defence Board was established but not greatly used.[11] Although not mentioned in the 1958 White Paper, perhaps the most significant aid to rational resource allocation among the services during this period was the introduction in the late 1950s of the annual five-year defence plan with detailed costings of major items of expenditure; the plan was to be developed in due course into a ten-year, long-term costing. Apart from this management tool, those concerned with a coherent defence policy and a rational allocation of resources would have for some years yet to rely more on the personalities of the Minister of Defence and the Chief of the Defence Staff than on the organisation set up to advise them.

THE MOUNTBATTEN REFORMS AND DEFENCE BY DISCUSSION

The next events that were to shape defence organisation were the arrival of Lord Mountbatten as Chief of the Defence Staff in early 1959 and the departure of Mr. Sandys in October of the same year. These two events (perhaps since the overlap was a matter of months they can be considered as a single event) coincided with intense pressure from all three Services for a change in the defence policy laid down in 1957. This period of the "Appeal Against Sandys"[12] should not intrude too far into a study of defence organisation; but it is important because it facilitated some crucial changes in defence organisation, paving the way for the 1964 reorganisation.

The relatively modest changes in organisation proposed by Lord Mountbatten were, according to reports,[13] opposed by the Service departments. Nevertheless, the post of Director of Defence Plans at brigadier level was created in September 1959 to chair the meetings of the three Service directors of plans (as the directors of the central defence policy staff were then called), and following Lord Mountbatten's appointment as Chief of the Defence Staff, his briefing staff was enlarged to about fifteen officers at colonel and lieutenant colonel levels drawn from all three Services. The post of Director of Defence Plans lasted through the 1964 reforms. The briefing staff have not survived in the same strength, but the importance of both in the period 1959–64 can hardly be overestimated. They were in many ways complementary to each other, and, equally important, they formed an essential element in the dialogue that is so vital in resource allocation. Those civil servants in the Ministry of Defence responsible for the defence budget now had Service colleagues at staff level with a loyalty to the Chief of the Defence Staff with whom resource allocation could be discussed. Hitherto, their military advice had come mainly if not exclusively from joint planning staffs who as "the conscious representatives of their Services"[14] had a primary and normally overriding loyalty to their own Service.

The foregoing is not to suggest that Service officers joining the CDS briefing staff (and later the central policy planning staffs) lost their Service loyalties; the loyalty to Service remained, but in their new position they would find it possible to recognise that sometimes their own Service would have to give way on an issue if logical argument and the military judgment of other Service colleagues required it. The position of a bureaucrat in an organisation will often dictate his judgments, or rather the extent to which he feels he can listen to and accept rational arguments.

These changes, small in size but of crucial importance, were, as has been said, resisted. It is doubtful whether they would have been accepted if all Services had been satisfied with the status quo. It was because all three Services desired to change the 1957 defence policy and to reallocate the defence budget that the nucleus of a central policy staff of Service officers and civil servants was formed. A forum for discussion had been created in which at least some of the participants, both Service and civilian, were not in a single-Service hierarchy. This process will be called Defence by Discussion to distinguish it from Defence by Bargaining. The essential ingredient in the new process was the increasingly dominant voice of the central defence organisation at all levels of defence planning from the Defence Minister downwards. If the central view prevails, then one would expect that a coherent defence policy would emerge, supported by a rational allocation of resources.

Few concerned with the subject in the late 1950s, whether in Whitehall or outside, felt that defence organisation had reached a final form. But debate concentrated as much on ways of improving the command and control of the Services in current operations as on effective long-term planning and efficient resource allocation. There also was a genuine fear that if planning and resource allocation were carried out in an organisation free from responsibility for day-to-day control of operations, then "irresponsible" planners would commit the nation to disastrous strategies. This concern has been characterised as the OKW argument[15] on the analogy, surely incorrect, of German experience in World War II. Those who pressed the argument probably gained added support from the Services' opinion of Mr. Sandys whom many considered to have been a one-man OKW. It was against this background that in 1962 the government appointed Lord Ismay and Sir Ian Jacob to report on future defence organisation; according to many accounts they paid close attention to Lord Mountbatten's views on this subject.[16]

THE 1964 REORGANISATION AND THE HEALEY ERA

The strong desire to link planning and day-to-day management in one organisation is reflected in the 1963 White Paper on Defence Organisation, which followed and largely implemented the Ismay-Jacob Report. The task of the Defence Ministry was defined for the first time: "to ensure effective coordination ... of all questions of policy and administration which concern the fighting Services as instruments of an effective strategy." The White Paper went on to point to the separation of policy staff in the Ministry of Defence from management staff in the Service departments as a major defect of the pre-1964 defence organisation.[17]

There is clearly not space here to deal adequately with the large-scale reshaping of defence organisation in 1964, the main outlines of which have been altered only once (by the addition of the Procurement Executive) since then. However, three points should be noted.

- First, the supreme authority of the Secretary of State for Defence (the new title of the Minister of Defence) was confirmed; the Service departments were merged into the Ministry of Defence, and their politically appointed ministers were subordinated to the Secretary of State who as time went on increasingly delegated across-the-board rather than single-Service responsibilities to them.

- Second, the position of the Chief of the Defence Staff, the Chiefs of Staff, and the joint planning staffs was not changed significantly, although they were to be supported in due course by four integrated organisations: the Defence Operations Executive, the Defence Signals Staff, the Defence Intelligence Staff, and the Defence Operational Requirements Staff. The fact that major changes were not made in the central defence planning organisation, which was becoming increasingly involved in resource allocation problems, says much for the 1957–59 reforms in this area.

- Third, the authority of the Permanent Secretary, the senior civil servant in the ministry was extended to cover all civil servants in the new combined ministry and parallel arrangements were made whereby the Chief Scientist could call on all scientific staff in the ministry for advice and information.

Thus all three parties to the resource allocation discussion—the military planners concerned with requirements, the civil servants concerned with the provision of resources, and the scientific staff, who if not themselves impartial (being human!) had access to the impartial techniques of mathematics and science—were relieved of at least some of the ties imposed by loyalty to a single-Service organisation. If Defence by Bargaining describes the pre-Sandys era, the 1964 reorganisation strengthened the tendency toward Defence by Discussion: there was now a strong central staff to devise guidelines for policy and to attempt by argument and discussion to arrange a rational allocation of defence resources.

Although Mr. Healey played no part in the 1964 reorganisation, largely complete before he came to office, his part in putting to use this new organisation and some of the new management techniques being developed in the United States is well known.[18] Defence by Discussion took on a fresh dimension when output budgeting (in the form of the functional costings) was introduced, and Mr. Healey was able to claim for the 1966 Defence Review that "for the first time in British history—machinery did not exist for this earlier—the cabinet was told what it would cost to adopt certain policies."[19] In addition, the Defence Operations Analysis Establishment (DOAE) was set up to undertake more extensive studies and to obtain an across-the-board view. Finally, in 1968 the joint planning staff took on a new role. They were given responsibility for preparing papers for the Chiefs of Staff on all issues of defence policy and relieved of responsibility for operational and contingency planning. Their new name, the defence policy staff, emphasised the change and also the requirement that members of it should not think of themselves solely as representatives of their own service.

But all was not plain sailing. Despite the changes just noted, 1965 and 1966 saw a furious controversy between the Navy and the Air Force Department over the need for a new aircraft carrier on which depended the future of organic fixed-wing air power with the Fleet. The Navy lost the argument and Mr. Christopher Mayhew, the minister of state responsible for the Navy, felt it necessary to resign in early 1966. In 1967, a further reorganisation took place at the top. The ministers of state in charge of the three Service departments were replaced by the more junior rank, parliamentary under-secretary of state. Two new ministers of state were created with functional, across-the-board, responsibilities; one to be in charge of administration and one for equipment. Each had one permanent secretary to assist him, and at the same time each of the Services lost their permanent secretaries who were replaced by deputy secretaries. As a result of these changes, functionalisation at the top was nearly complete. Figure 3.1 illustrates the complex chain of authority at the end of the 1960s. A subsequent decision was made to reorganise the top civil-service structure so that there was, outside the Procurement Executive (to be considered later), one permanent secretary and one second permanent secretary (administration). This decision did not impair the principle that, with the exception of the three parliamentary under-secretary posts, all political and top civil service posts had functional, across-the-board, rather than single-service responsibilities.

THE 1970s AND AFTER

The final step toward functionalisation at the top was taken in 1981, when after another hard-fought defence review in which significant reductions in the future surface fleet were enforced, the Parliamentary Under Secretary for the Navy, Mr. Keith Speed, spoke against the cuts and had to resign. The three single-Service parliamentary under-secretary posts were replaced by two posts at the same level reporting respectively to the Minister of State for Defence (Armed Forces) and the Minister of State for Defence (Defence Procurement).

Some months later, as if to prove the adage that "tough defence reviews breed tough defence reorganisations," it became known that the position of the Chief of the Defence Staff had been further enhanced. He was identified as the government's principal military adviser able to offer independent advice, which might well differ from that which he would have to offer as Chairman of the Chiefs of Staff. These changes were reported to the House of Commons Defence Committee in early 1982.[20] More details were revealed when the holder of a new post, Deputy Chief of the Defence Staff, briefed the press on 16 September 1982. His subsequent lecture to the Royal United Services Institute for Defence Studies on 12 October 1983 in London gave a complete description of the new organisation.[21] He explained that he was to take charge of the central defence staff, formerly the defence policy staff, the successors to the joint planning staff.[22] This staff would in the future be divided into two groups, one advising on commitments (broadly speaking the likely theatres of operations in any future war) and the other on programmes; the later group would advise on exactly those items President Truman mentioned in the 1945 message to Congress quoted at the head of chapter 1, that is, strategy, (weapons) programmes, and (the defence) budget.

The overwhelming importance of decisions in resource allocation had never been recognised so decisively in previous reorganisations. In the future, these staffs would be responsible for providing independent advice to the Chief of the Defence Staff rather than forming part of a bargaining process in which each Service sought to protect its own interests. Figure 3.2 showing the whole higher defence organisation in 1982 uses a grid pattern to illustrate the dual interlocking responsibilities of most senior staff. Outside observers were no doubt surprised to learn that some eighteen years after the 1964 reorganisation, changes were still necessary to prevent the Services from reverting to Defence by Bargaining. More difficulties come to light when the evolution of the Procurement Executive is considered.

In 1971, after a report by Mr. Derek Rayner (as he then was), the government decided to set up a self-contained organisation, responsible to the Secretary of State for Defence, for procuring weapons and equipment, and most stores, for all three Services. This action brought to an end a policy started in 1939, under which procurement decisions for either the Army or Air Force, or both, were taken by another government department outside the defence area. In the future the head of the Procurement Executive would be a civil servant, not a politician, and he would have three systems controllers for sea, land, and air weapons systems, and a fourth responsible for guided weapons and electronics across-the-board. Each controller would be an accounting officer directly responsible to Parliament (like the permanent secretaries in the major government departments) for the expenditure on his vote. The new organisation was designed to be independent and free from single-Service blinkers.

However, what Richard Hastie Smith calls a process of "constructive erosion" took place.[23] Numerous changes have been effected since 1971, but as important as any for defence policymaking was the abolition of the controllerate for guided missiles and electronics. Thereafter, as Hastie Smith says, "the identification of the systems controllers with their Service boards [the committees corporately responsible for each Service department] became virtually complete"; but he goes on to point out that the drift of power back to the Service departments, which was apparent in the evolution of the Procurement Executive, owed much to circumstances outside the Ministry of Defence, notably the introduction in 1969 of the annual Public Expenditure White Papers. To appreciate Hastie Smith's point, a fuller description is needed of current procedures for allocating defence resources between competing claims.

DEFENCE POLICYMAKING TODAY

The heart of the process is long-term costing, which the ministry prepares annually to set out in vote or input format the cost of its plans for ten years ahead. The start of these costing procedures in the 1950s has already been noted, but it was only during the 1960s that they were fully developed and used for more sophisticated exercises in resource allocation. Finally, in 1969 the first Public Expenditure White Paper was published, giving all major government departments long-term financial targets on which to base their future policies.

The defence costings are prepared annually on the basis of policy assumptions agreed centrally in the Ministry of Defence.[24] The target for defence expenditure is derived from the previous year's Public Expenditure Survey, which sets ceilings on government expenditure in all its main areas of activity, including defence, for the next three years or so. Within this framework, the defence long-term costings are worked out by the Service departments and the Procurement Executive at the start of the year so that by the summer the costings can be fitted into the current year's Public Expenditure Survey which will advance the targets by one more year. By the autumn, with the costings approved by the government, defence estimates are prepared for the coming financial year which starts in April, and assumptions for the next year's costings are prepared at the same time so that the whole process can start again. The connection of the long-term costings to the Public Expenditure Survey, which should commit the government to a particular level of expenditure for some years ahead, provides a sound framework for planning with a reasonable assurance that sufficient funds will be available in the first three to five years and with some flexibility in allocations in the second five years of the costing period. The introduction of cash limits procedures for the financial year 1976–77 was intended to be an addition to rather than a fundamental change in these procedures. Chapters 9 and 13 consider further the extent to which high inflation and cash limits have distorted financial planning.

Even if the process of allocating funds to defence and other government activities seems broadly satisfactory, serious doubts still exist about the effectiveness of the machinery for allocating funds among various activities within the defence field. From the inception of the costings procedures, defence targets for future years have, broadly speaking, been suballotted to individual Service departments for detailed financial planning and control. This procedure was probably inevitable in the circumstances because as Hastie Smith points out, only the Service departments had sufficient knowledge of the detailed and intricate interrelationships of their weapons programmes to cut and mould them into the shapes necessary to conform with the subtargets. It is true that the programme changes which they proposed had to be endorsed by the Chiefs of Staff and approved by the Secretary of State and that endorsement and approval were by no means a formality. But, he concludes, "the task was a very large and complex one and in general this was essentially a situation in which knowledge was power."[25] So wrote a civil servant from the Ministry of Defence in 1975, and he would no doubt agree that the increasingly unfavorable financial climate for defence expenditure since then has increased the power of the Service departments vis-a-vis the centre.

When targets for future expenditures have to be cut, often in a hurry, the cuts tend to be applied to all readily accessible programmes. The main cuts imposed on defence expenditure by successive governments have normally been passed on, broadly pro rata, to the Service departments, which have been left to absorb them as best they can. This process is the heart of the matter to which this study will return more than once. When funds are scarce, the Secretary of State for Defence is almost bound under present arrangements to look to the Service departments, his main management units, to spend funds wisely and provide prudently for future commitments. The Service departments in their turn, unless firmly and unequivocally directed otherwise, will tend to spare programmes and projects that they see as vital to the interests of their Service, even if their views do not wholly accord with overall defence policy.

Another commentator, David Greenwood, categorizes this process as one of "suboptimisation." If the current method of defence budgeting is any improvement upon Defence by Bargaining, it can only be to the extent that, to quote Greenwood again, "The broad structure of defence priorities is decided upon by the central policy staffs whose task it is to consider the nation's strategic objectives and the role of military power in support of them. . . . These ideas may be behind any special studies and reviews that may be made"—by the Defence Operational Analysis Establishment and similar establishments—"and equipment proposals are considered in the light of them."[26]

RETROSPECT

It is worth pausing for a moment to note the somewhat surprising evolution in procedures for resource allocation decisionmaking since 1946. Then, resource allocation decisions were the responsibility of the individual Service departments, and such decisions as were to be made in favour of one Service or the other were made by civilians; that is, either by ministers or by civil servants in the Treasury or Service departments or both. This process reached its limit in the 1957 White Paper where one civilian, Mr. Sandys, shaped the policy and made the decisions. Admittedly these decisions were made after discussion with the Chiefs of Staff, but the final outcome caused serious misgivings in at least one of them. The situation is different now. The machinery for putting together the long-term defence budget and allocating resources within the defence field is large and complex. The central civilian staffs concerned with programmes and budget play a crucial role, but the Service departments, the defence policy staffs, the scientific staffs, and ultimately the Chief of the Defence Staff all play essential parts in recommending the final allocation to ministers.

The foregoing is not to argue that a Secretary of State cannot still play a decisive role in defence policymaking, particularly if he decides to set firm guidelines and adjust financial targets accordingly before a special defence review (or the annual long-term costing) begins.[27] The difference between the Sandys era and the present is the extent to which the Secretary of State has military and civilian staffs at the centre with the authority and experience to assist him in formulating his directives and ensuring compliance with them.

The evolution of a central organisation for defence in the United Kingdom has passed through three stages that, if not seen as distinct at the time, are identifiable as being so in retrospect. First came Defence by Bargaining from 1904 to 1957, when coordination not control of the Services was the paramount aim. The creation of a Ministry of Defence in 1946 can be seen in retrospect to be the culmination of that phase. Possibly Mr. Attlee's experience of the wartime machinery of government was an important element in the decision to create a super-secretariat rather than a super-ministry.[28] Insofar as resource allocation decisions were concerned, that was the era of Defence by Bargaining between the Services. The second and shortest phase began in 1957, when a supposedly final defence policy with a radical reallocation of roles between the Services was laid down by the minister in charge of defence, Mr. Sandys.

Finally, the departure of Mr. Sandys in 1959 saw the start of a still-continuing process that might be called Defence by Discussion: through successive reorganisations, increasing emphasis has been placed on discussion and analysis by the Defence Policy Staff in conjunction with the civilian staffs of the Permanent Under-Secretary and the Chief Scientific Adviser to achieve a rational allocation of the resources allotted to defence.

However, Defence by Bargaining and Defence by Discussion are not black and white, clearly definable, and easily distinguishable from each other. Organisations are composed of complex interacting systems that change over time. The best one can do is identify at any one time a tendency toward one style of defence management or the other. This style may change when new people (such as a new Defence Secretary) or new techniques or structures are introduced. It would appear, however, that the United Kingdom has gone a long way toward devising an organisation capable of making an objective assessment of defence priorities and allocating the available defence budget in the light of this assessment. If this organisation is not sufficient to achieve a coherent defence policy, then some alternative methods, discussed in chapters 12 and 13 may have to be considered to achieve the desired result.

Chapter Four

Central Defence Organisation in the United States

BACKGROUND

The history of the central organisation for defence in the United States is shorter than that of its counterpart in the United Kingdom, but can in a sense be said to derive from the same root and have had at the start the same philosophy of Defence by Bargaining. The divergence of the two systems in the forty years or so since World War II is therefore all the more remarkable.

ORIGINS

Before World War II a joint Army and Navy Board handled inter-Service matters, but it was not until 1942, when it was decided to establish a supreme Anglo-American military body for the strategic direction of the war, that the Joint Chiefs of Staff (JCS) were created. Until the end of the war, they sat as colleagues of and counterparts to the existing British Chiefs of Staff Committee, and both from all accounts functioned in a similar fashion. The position of the Joint Chiefs of Staff was not formalised, however, until 1947 when the National Security Act also set up the Department of the Air Force, created the post of the Secretary of Defense, and authorised the appointment of a small military and civilian staff to serve the Secretary.

Between 1944 and 1947, there was much discussion of the form the new central defence organisation should take and, in contrast to the United Kingdom at that time, there was strong pressure, notably from the Army and the Air Corps,[1] for one chief of staff reporting directly to the President and for one secretary for the armed forces. This proposal was resisted by Mr. Forrestal, the Secretary of the Navy, who pressed for three separate Service departments with a Secretary of Defense over all.

THE 1947 AND 1949 REORGANISATIONS

After two years of intense debate in the Senate Committee on Military Affairs and elsewhere both in Congress and in the executive, the final decision was embodied in the National Security Act of 1947. Congress, mindful of the separation of powers embodied in the Constitution, was clearly unwilling to grant too much power to the executive by creating a single department for defence affairs. Nevertheless, the financial savings that could stem from unification were obviously attractive. The solution, therefore, was not one department but four, a Secretary of Defense and three Service departments, the former exercising "general direction, authority, and control" over the latter; but Congress retained the right to question each Service separately about its proposals for expenditure. The Joint Chiefs of Staff were formally recognised and the National Security Council (NSC) was set up to advise the President on the integration of domestic, foreign, and military policies relating to national security.

This solution was clearly a compromise. The Secretary of Defense presided over "a weak confederation of military units,"[2] rather than the single unified department originally proposed by the Army, and yet it was a significant step toward that objective. The National Security Council and the Central Intelligence Agency had been brought into being, and the Secretary was given staff to help him in coordinating the activities of the Services to eliminate waste and duplication in logistic support and to supervise the budget. Figure 4.1 illustrates the position but, as charts must, it fails to show the extent to which the Service departments had freedom to act as they thought best.

In comparison with the British Ministry of Defence, however, which was during this period a ministry almost entirely devoted to coordination, the US Department of Defense had some powers at least to control the Services. Perhaps one of the reasons for the difference between the two systems lies in the different circumstances surrounding their births. In the United States there was a vigorous public debate in which extreme solutions were discussed, after which a compromise was adopted. In the United Kingdom there was far less debate outside the corridors of power.

The defects in the new organisation showed up, not surprisingly, when problems of resource allocation began to appear. Mr. Forrestal, former Secretary of the Navy and the first Secretary of Defense, wished to act as a coordinator. His "constant impulse was to understand and adjust rather than to rush to conclusions and issue orders,"[3] but he faced great difficulties in 1948 and 1949 when the defence budgets were being prepared. He received little help from the Joint Chiefs of Staff either in preparing these budgets on a realistic basis or in allocating the cuts enforced by President Truman on the "necessary minimum" budgets proposed by the Services.

After the 1948 communist coup in Czechoslovakia, President Truman called for a supplementary defence budget. The Joint Chiefs of Staff suggested a supplement of $9 billion; Mr. Forrestal reduced this arbitrarily to $3.48 billion before submitting it to the White House. President Truman finally accepted a maximum of $3.17 billion. The same balance-the-budget philosophy dominated the formulation of the 1950 budget. Its ceiling was fixed by President Truman at $14.4 billion, "apparently without consulting the JCS or NSC,"[4] and Mr. Forrestal made the initial allocation among the Services himself because, despite his best efforts to enlist JCS aid in making this decision, they remained adamant that $16.9 billion was the minimum.

This experience, among others, led Mr. Forrestal to consider major changes in the 1947 legislation as early as the summer of 1948. He told the Senate Armed Services Committee just before his death in 1949 that "after having viewed the problem at close range for the past 18 months, I must admit to you quite frankly that my position on the question has changed. I am now convinced that there are adequate checks and balances inherent in our governmental structure to prevent misuse of the broad authority which I feel must be vested in the Secretary of Defense."[5] This public change of position by a leading opponent of greater unification clearly paved the way for increased powers for the Secretary of Defense, and the 1949 amendments to the National Security Act represented a major step in the direction of unification.[6] The Service departments were merged into the Department of Defense, which became an executive department. The Secretary of Defense was given full control over the Service departments, but Congress laid down that the Services were still to be separately administered. The Secretary of Defense was given a deputy to assist him, and the key officials in what would soon be called the Office of the Secretary of Defense (OSD) were upgraded and their staffs increased. Finally, the position of Chairman of the Joint Chiefs of Staff was created. Despite these changes in organisation, the Services retained sufficient independence to practise Defence by Bargaining unless a strong Secretary of Defense backed by his President was determined to intervene. Figure 4.2 illustrates the new position.

THE ROLE OF THE SECRETARY OF DEFENSE

It would be convenient, but misleading, to see changes in the organisation of the Department of Defense between 1949 and 1961 as entailing a steady increase in the power of the Secretary of Defense and a gradual unification of the department. In fact, the style of defence policymaking in the period (and indeed subsequently) was dictated to a large extent by the wishes of the President and his Secretary of Defense; the actual changes in the organisation of the department had much less influence than for instance in the United Kingdom where a permanent bureaucracy has more control over how business is done.

A Secretary of Defense might, like Mr. Forrestal, see himself as having authority and responsibilities similar to those of a British cabinet minister. In this role he would be responsible for initiating policy and would suggest and secure presidential approval for a total for the defence budget which he would then share out between the Services, if possible with their consent, and, if not, by imposing a solution with the President's backing. There were clear limitations to the comparison with British cabinet ministers, as President Truman pointed out,[7] but nonetheless this concept of the role of the Secretary of Defense as one of policymaking was a valid and workable one which others beside Mr. Forrestal followed.

At the other extreme would be a Secretary of Defense like Mr. Wilson who concentrated more on managing the Department of Defense and resolving administrative problems within it. It would be fair to argue that he left policymaking, including the major decisions on strategy and resource allocation among the Services, to President Eisenhower. As a result, the President, the Secretary of State, and the White House advisers became the focal point of policy, and the Secretary of Defense became the agent in executing it. Mr. Nelson Rockefeller, who advised President Eisenhower about defence organisation on numerous occasions between 1953 and 1958, supported this view of the role of the Secretary of Defense.[8]

James Roherty, who first pointed out these two alternative roles for a Secretary of Defense, has argued that each Secretary of Defense before Mr. McNamara can be categorised as either a generalist like Mr. Forrestal or a functionalist like Mr. Wilson.[9] For the purposes of this study, one need not accept Professor Roherty's argument at all points; one should realise, however, that these changes in the style of defence policymaking, however frequently or infrequently they occurred, did nothing to diminish the authority and independence of the Service departments. They had little incentive to surrender any of their powers so long as any defence policy involving a reallocation of defence resources that was agreed to by the Joint Chiefs of Staff and Service departments could be overruled by a President, such as President Eisenhower, who would then impose his own policy and allocate resources to carry it out, whatever the reservations of one or more of the Services. Moreover, the fact that the style of defence policymaking to be adopted depended largely on the wishes of the President and his Secretary of Defense, discouraged the permanent bureaucracy from trying to reorganise itself to produce a more unified defence policy. Unless a strong President and Secretary of Defense made strenuous efforts to impose a defence solution, the three Services were likely to revert to Defence by Bargaining.

THE 1953 AND 1958 REORGANISATIONS

The 1953 reorganisation gave more powers both to the Secretary of Defense and to the Chairman of the Joint Chiefs of Staff. But these powers were not sufficient, and in 1958, "faced by continuing interservice rivalry and competition about the development and control of strategic weapons,"[10] Congress agreed to further changes in the defence organisation. The authority of the Secretary of Defense over the Service departments was again confirmed, and the authority of the Chairman of the Joint Chiefs of Staff was increased. Other important changes in the operational command structure were also made, as a result of which the chain of operational command ran from the President through the Secretary of Defense and the Joint Chiefs of Staff direct to the unified and specified commands of the armed forces.

Considerable as these changes were, they did not produce clear guidance for the formulation of defence policy. General Taylor told the Senate Subcommittee on National Policy Machinery in 1960, "the Joint Chiefs of Staff have often been at odds over what is expected of the armed forces and have been unable to agree on the size and composition of forces needed to provide the military component of national strategy."[11] Consequently, the budget ceilings, "often set with little knowledge of their strategic implications," controlled the growth, direction, and evolution of the armed forces and gave "economic and budgetary factors an overriding say in determining military posture." It was against this background of continued Defence by Bargaining that Mr. McNamara became Secretary of Defense in 1961.

THE McNAMARA ERA

Mr. McNamara was determined from the start to avoid a passive role as Secretary of Defense that would involve merely judging on recommendations put to him; instead, he wished to exercise active leadership: probing, suggesting alternatives, and proposing objectives for defence policy. He decided that new management methods, which had been developed mainly on a theoretical basis, would be more useful in achieving his aim than a further reorganisation of the Department of Defense.[12] Consequently, the study of US defence organisation between 1961 and 1968 must pay more attention to management techniques than to bureaucratic structures.

The Planning, Programming, and Budgeting System (PPBS), or output budgeting, is rightly the best known of the McNamara reforms. It is in a sense the most basic and probably the most generally acceptable of them. Since 1956, the Joint Chiefs of Staff had produced an annual Joint Strategic Objectives Plan covering the level of forces and the major programmes proposed for the following five years, but hitherto this plan had consisted of a series of single-Service plans that were not coordinated or compressed within an attainable overall budget. Mr. Hitch, who became Comptroller in 1961, subsequently commented on this gap between planning and budgeting. He suggested that before the introduction of the PPB system, the main method used by civilians (including Defense Secretaries in this term) to bridge this gap "was to divide a total defense budget ceiling among the three military departments, leaving each department by and large the allocation of its ceiling among its own functions, units, and activities" because "they lacked the management techniques needed to do it any other way."[13] It is hard to accept that things were quite as bad as he suggests: the imposition of the New Look doctrine and the outcome of the Thor/Jupiter controversy over strategic missiles show that the Services did not have complete freedom to spend their allocation as they wished. But Mr. Hitch is right to suggest the absence of close coordination between planning and budgeting. The PPB system was designed to remedy this defect.

After his appointment as Comptroller in 1961, Mr. Hitch introduced the new procedure which amounted in effect to a continuing pattern of work affecting all stages of the planning and resource allocation process. It started when the Joint Strategic Objectives Plan was submitted to the Secretary of Defense in the spring. The Secretary's review produced tentative force guidance on which the military staff produced the five-year force structure and financial programme. The major areas of review would be covered by a Draft Presidential Memorandum prepared in the offices of either the Deputy for Systems Analysis or the Director for Defense Research and Engineering. Then followed the all important reconciliation of planning and budgeting based on the functions, outputs, or program elements of the plan. These elements were the basic building blocks of the whole package and were designed on the basis that "the unifying principle underlying each major program is a common mission or set of purposes for the elements involved" (see table 9.1).[14]

Clearly, output budgeting can be of great assistance in making a rational allocation of defence resources, but does not necessarily help the decisionmaker choose between two weapons systems designed to achieve the same end and therefore presumably to be funded from the same program. It is here that the second and perhaps less understood of the McNamara reforms comes into play. From 1961 onwards, increasing use was made of quantitative techniques drawn from mathematics, statistics, and economics to help in the choice between options. These techniques have a number of names of which "systems analysis" is the most well known.[15]

Systems analysis attempts to calculate the effectiveness of a complete weapon system in operation against a rational and responsive adversary.

One early study based on a systems approach was the Hickey Study of 1961. This study was ultimately developed into an analytical system for assessing strategic nuclear force requirements comprehending US Strategic Retaliatory Forces, Continental Air and Missile Defence Forces, and Civil Defence Forces in one inter-Service model.[16] The study started by calculating how many of the planned weapons systems would be needed in service to destroy 75 percent and 90 percent of all strategic targets. This estimate was then combined with the objective laid down by Mr. McNamara that the US strategic nuclear deterrent should be able to destroy 50 percent of the industry and 25 percent of the population of the Soviet Union. As a result, subsequent studies were able to restate the problem "how much is enough deterrence" in such a way that all the component parts—such as strategic forces, ABMs, and civil defence—fell into place and the problem could be put into a numerically based system in which alternative hypotheses could be tested. It is hard to see how purposeful Strategic Arms Limitation Talks could have taken place without such studies as the Hickey Study and related thinking. The initiative for these studies was clearly Mr. McNamara's successful effort to force those concerned to think quantitatively.

The merits and defects of these new techniques are not relevant at this stage, but the way in which they were used in the Department of Defense in the 1960s had a considerable effect on the conduct of defence business and must be considered further. As the brief description of the Hickey Study has shown, the initiative lay with the Secretary of Defense who frequently used Draft Presidential Memoranda as a means of starting debate. These papers were normally written in the Office of the Secretary of Defense, probably by the Systems Analysis Office. They were then circulated to the Service departments who were expected to challenge them if necessary and submit alternative proposals. Often, debate was thus initiated by the Secretary, but he would sometimes fail to recognise that given the prestige of his office and the power of the analysis used, it was debate on subjects of his own choosing and on his terms. He had the initiative, and through the year or so of preparation and discussion before the summary memorandum to the President was ready, any Service disagreeing with the policy outlined might well find it impossible to widen the debate or pose a radical reformulation of the question.

In effect, a policy of active management allied to the new management methods gave rise to a situation that James Roherty has summarised as follows: "A policy framework is set by the Secretary; much of the data base is provided by the Secretary; judgments are invited by the Secretary; decisions are made by the Secretary."[17] Professor Roherty's succinct description may not do full justice to the considerable discussion that the staff in the Office of the Secretary of Defense would have with their opposite numbers in the Service departments or to the fact that these discussions did, on occasion, change the guidelines of debate. But he rightly stresses that this was management from the top with ideas and initiatives coming from there rather than from the main organisation itself (that is, from the Joint Chiefs of Staff or the Service departments). Defence by Bargaining was succeeded by a new form of management in which decisions were preceded by a debate in which only one person, the Secretary of Defense, had a vote. The ability to reformulate basic and apparently insoluble questions, such a vital need in the advance of scientific or philosophical thought, is certainly eroded in debate of this nature between unequals.

The consequences for the US Department of Defense were important. Mr. McNamara very properly wished to secure a thorough debate of alternatives, objectives, and costs, and, to be effective, that this debate should be continuous with all criteria in the analysis of options being made explicit. This encouragement of an adversary procedure must have served to strengthen the feeling in each of the three Service departments that they must retain the maximum independence. In his foreword to the Report of the Blue Ribbon Defense Panel on the Department of Defense, the chairman wrote in 1970: "The Panel found many things it believes should be corrected, but it believes, and I agree, that many of the difficulties result from the structure of the Department of Defense itself which almost inevitably leads people into 'adversary' relationships rather than toward cooperation in the interests of the Department—and the nation—as a whole."[18]

THE NIXON-FORD ERA

Mr. Nixon's administration took office with a commitment to change the previous methods of carrying out defence business,[19] and in his 1971 Statement on Defense Posture, Mr. Laird wrote that he "inherited a system designed for highly centralized decisionmaking. Overcentralization in so large an organization leads to a kind of paralysis. Many decisions are not made at all or, if they are made, lack full coordination and commitment by those who must implement the decisions."[20] Participatory management was to be the watchword of the Laird era, and a number of changes in the procedures were made in order to give effect to this management style.

These procedures need not be considered in detail, but the overall effects can be appreciated from a brief mention of one of them. In 1971, Mr. Laird ensured that at an early stage in the planning-budgeting cycle the Joint Chiefs of Staff and the Service departments were given better guidance for five years ahead on which to plan. As a result, the "JCS had to develop force structures within stated money ceilings provided early in the planning and budgeting process. The Services could then plan, knowing how much money they could count on and could make internal decisions about how to allocate resources against overall priorities."[21]

In effect, therefore, the initiative in the planning process was passed back to the Services, and the Office of the Secretary of Defense, including the Office of Systems Analysis, became, after budget guidance had been given, a reviewing rather than an initiating organisation; it reacted to the initiatives of the Services rather than seeking to control which new ideas should be followed up and which should be ignored. The Services accepted the overall level of the defence budget and in return were reasonably free to suballocate their share as they thought fit. The Service departments very much appreciated this change; in consequence, Mr. Laird must have found it much easier to manage the drastic reductions in both force levels and budgets that occurred as a result of the US withdrawal from Vietnam. There are interesting similarities between this approach and the UK system of absorbing severe cuts in the defence budget in the 1970s.

Although there were no major changes in organisation within the Department of Defense at the start of the Nixon administration, considerable changes in governmental organisation outside the Pentagon had a significant effect on defence. In particular, Mr. Nixon changed the status and doubled the staff of the National Security Council, and created under it the Defense Program Review Committee with the intention that "decisions not only on the total size of the defense budget but also on major programs will be made outside the Pentagon in an interagency forum where White House influence is dominant."[22] Although major strategy was settled by the National Security Council, the extent to which this power was actually used to intervene in the resource allocation process when Mr. Laird was at the Pentagon, or later, is open to doubt. But it is important to stress that both the power to intervene and the staff to make this intervention effective were established by these reforms and could be so used in the future.

Another notable initiative by the Nixon administration in this field was the establishment of the Blue Ribbon Defense Panel of sixteen nonmilitary members to advise on defence organisation. Their report issued in 1970 was critical and in important areas echoed the remarks by the chairman already quoted. The following quotation is of particular interest:

> The evolution of defence organization since 1947 has not substantially reduced the inherent difficulties arising from the fact that the division of roles and missions among the military departments is still based fundamentally on distinctions between land, sea, and air forces which have become increasingly less relevant. This results in continued adversary relations between the military services, which although usually confined to the internal paper wars that constitute the department's decisionmaking process, severely inhibit the achievement of economy and effectiveness required for adequate defense

> within available resources. The continuing interservice competition seriously degrades the decisionmaking process through obfuscation of issues and alternatives and leads to attempts to circumvent decisions, repeated efforts to reopen issues that have already been decided, and slow, unenthusiastic implementation of policies to which a service objects.

The report goes on to cite as examples of this parochialism "the development of the AX aircraft by the Air Force and the Cheyenne aircraft by the Army for the close air-support role, the lack of enthusiasm for airlift by the Air Force and the fast deployment logistics programme by the Navy, both intended to support the Army, and the continued failure to resolve the issue of the best balance between land- and carrier-based tactical air."[23]

However, the reforms that the panel suggested to counter these defects were not implemented. The reforms would have involved the relinquishment by the Joint Chiefs of Staff of any concern with current military operations and the establishment of a deputy secretary of defense to be responsible for the evaluation of weapons systems and finance. The deputy secretary of defense for evaluation would have been supported by three assistant secretaries of defense; one of these would have been the Comptroller (responsible for budgeting), one would have covered program and force analysis (the former Office of Systems Analysis) and the third would have been responsible for test and evaluation of weapons systems. Clearly, this deputy secretary would have been a most powerful figure in the department, and it will be necessary to consider in chapter 10 the difficulties that can arise because of the gap between planning (by Systems Analysis) and budgeting (by the Comptroller), which under this proposal would have been eliminated.

It would be wrong to assume that the McNamara revolution had no lasting effects. On the contrary, the increased staff and expertise in the Office of the Secretary of Defense and the continuation of the PPB system gave later Secretaries of Defense some capability to intervene in the weapons acquisition process. Nevertheless, the Services have since then normally retained the autonomy over resource allocation that was part of participatory management, and Defence by Bargaining is still a valid description of that process. Sometimes it seemed as if the Secretary of Defense had to bargain or negotiate with the Services as, for instance, when he would propose extra funds for a Service to develop a weapon which he supported; but the basic bargain was the one struck between the three Services. Each Service agreed not to interfere in the budget decisions of the other two provided that it was free to spend its own share as it thought best.

Mr. Laird's successor, Mr. Elliot Richardson, was only in post for a few months. There is good reason to believe that he would have wanted to make some changes either in organisation or in procedures so that defence decisionmaking could be made more rational.[24] Mr. Schlesinger, who replaced Mr. Richardson in 1973, did not make any major changes in defence organisation although some remarks in his 1974 report to Congress[25] show that he was well aware of the dangers of inter-Service rivalry over the share out of the defence budget. During his two years in office, he used the existing system, including the PPB system, rather than attempting another reorganisation. During much of his tenure, he was more concerned with opposing what he considered to be ill-advised cuts in the total defence budget than with intervening in the suballocations within his own department. He was replaced in 1975 by Mr. Rumsfeld who accepted the defence cuts opposed by his predecessor and supported the existing organisation, procedures, and policies.

Despite their differences in approach and the wide range of problems facing them, the Secretaries of Defense in the Nixon-Ford era accepted the organisation and budget systems they inherited from Mr. McNamara, but did not use them to intervene actively in the resource allocation process. In consequence, the Office of Systems Analysis declined in importance, and the assistant secretary post in charge of it was downgraded, but the directorate itself still survives with a more modest role. Perhaps in retrospect the most significant change in the longer term was the increased involvement of the National Security Council in resource allocation problems, following the creation of the Defense Program Review Committee.

THE CARTER PRESIDENCY

Three significant organisational changes were made during President Carter's term of office. The appointment in 1978 of the Commandant of the Marine Corps as a permanent member of the Joint Chiefs of Staff formalised what had long been the de facto position, because for many years prior to 1978 the Commandant had the right to attend JCS meetings when matters relevant to the Marine Corps were being discussed, a very wide remit. The notable feature for a foreign observer of US defence is that this change was made on the initiative of Congress, not the executive. Two new under-secretary posts were also created within the Office of the Secretary of Defense, one for policy and one for research and engineering. Figure 4.3 illustrates the position after these changes. It shows that the head of Program Analysis and Evaluation was once more an assistant secretary. The post was again downgraded by the incoming Reagan administration, but few other structural changes were made at that time.

Finally, the Defense Resources Board was set up in April 1979 under the chairmanship of the Deputy Secretary of Defense with the Secretaries of the Navy, Army, and Air Force and the Chairman of the Joint Chiefs of Staff among its members. The Board's task was and is to advise the Secretary of Defense on the allocation of resources. Its creation has not solved the fundamental problems noted so far in this study.

Clearly, however, the President's most important intervention in the resource allocation process was the cancellation of the B1 bomber programme. At first it seemed that despite presidential campaign promises of defence cuts the Pentagon's budget would survive relatively unscathed. When the administration presented its first budget of $120.37 billion, only $2.77 billion less than planned, many must have assumed that the President and Mr. Harold Brown, his Secretary of Defense, were not going to "rock the boat." The decision to cancel the B1, when announced in June 1977, certainly took many by surprise and caused an uproar among the supporters of the aircraft in the Pentagon, in Congress, and in industry. This is not the place to discuss the merits or demerits of the decision (later reversed by President Reagan). The important point for this study is to note that the decision, although fully supported by the Secretary of Defense, was made outside the Defense Department and apart from congressional debate and pressure. It was in essence a presidential decision rather than one evolved by consent after discussion within the Joint Chiefs of Staff or Department of Defense.

Soon after the B1 decision, the President directed his Secretary of Defense to conduct a searching organisational review of the Department of Defense. Mr. Brown's response to the presidential directive was to commission five reviews known collectively as the Defense Organization Study of 1977–80 (DOS 77.80) of which the most relevant for defence policymakers were those on Departmental Headquarters (the Ignatius Study), Defense Resource Management (the Rice Study), and the National Military Command (the Steadman Study). All five reports were published and elicited extensive comments from those affected. It is not possible to summarize neatly the thrust of so many reports that overlap in their concern for defence policymaking, but Archie Barrett[26] stresses that the findings and recommendations of these studies do in fact question the capability of the Department of Defense to plan. They recognise, as did the Blue Ribbon Defense Panel almost a decade earlier, that the dominating organisations in the Department of Defense are the Office of the Secretary of Defense and the Service departments, and that the JCS organisation does not play a full part as a corporate body within the department. In particular, the Joint Chiefs of Staff do not provide military advice on major issues detached from Service interests. Instead, the organisation acts as a forum in which each Service seeks to maximise its position through bargaining at each level in the process.

LATER DEVELOPMENTS

Despite these criticisms, no further major changes in defence organisation or resource allocation procedures were made either by President Carter[27] or by President Reagan[28] before a new and surprising turn of events occurred in 1982. Shortly before his retirement as Chairman of the Joint Chiefs of Staff, General David C. Jones, US Air Force, announced in the February 1982 edition of the *Directors and Boards Magazine* that he saw major faults in the JCS organisation.[29] The article was substantially reproduced in *Armed Forces Journal International* where it no doubt reached a wider Service audience. In the article, General Jones cogently argued the case against the current organisation on the grounds of (a) diffused responsibility and authority, (b) inadequate corporate advice on major issues, (c) dominance of the Joint Chiefs of Staff by individual Services, and (d) basic contradictions in the role of the Service chiefs as JCS members and as heads of Service. His recommendations, which included strengthening the position of the Chairman of the Joint Chiefs of Staff, making him wholly responsible for the joint staffs, bore a striking resemblance to those implemented without publicity by the British Secretary of State for Defence a short time before.

These forthright criticisms by an insider were extraordinary enough to arouse interest in Congress and the press, but perhaps as remarkable as anything to the outside observer was that the serving Army Chief of Staff, General E. C. Meyer, US Army, supported General Jones' criticisms and suggested even more radical solutions. The subsequent hearings of the House Armed Services Investigations Subcommittee produced a wide measure of support for the criticisms voiced by these two officers and a number of other solutions to the problems posed. These and the possible need for complementary changes elsewhere in the Department of Defense are discussed in later chapters. For the present, it is sufficient to note that the criticisms of the present organisation and of the process of defence resource allocation received striking endorsement from unimpeachable sources, very shortly after the presidential decision on the B1 bomber seemed to herald the continued success of Defence by Bargaining.

RETROSPECT

Despite the major organisational changes debated and initiated between 1945 and 1958 in the United States, the style and content of defence policymaking depend very much on the President and his Secretary of Defense. If the Secretary is so minded, and he has the backing of his President, major defence policy decisions can be taken by the executive despite the serious reservations and doubts among the heads of the Armed Services concerned. But in the absence of either a President like Mr. Eisenhower, able to impose strategic doctrine and possibly budget cuts upon a doubtful Army and Navy, or a Secretary of Defense like Mr. McNamara able, with presidential backing, to decide how the defence budget should be allocated, defence resource allocation will normally be effected by a system of Defence by Bargaining. Clearly, defence organisation has developed along rather different lines in the United Kingdom and the United States. The next two chapters examine the organisation of government in the two countries to see whether this can provide a satisfactory reason for these different methods of managing the defence resource allocation process.

Chapter Five
Structure: The Executive

THE RULES OF THE GAME

> Participation in the decision process does not occur at random. There are numerous written and unwritten rules governing how an issue may enter the system, who can become involved, who must be consulted, etc. The rules of the game are devices for ordering how minds are brought to bear on a problem. Some rules derive from the constitutional and legislative delegation of power. Others are spelled out in executive orders and other executive documents. An unwritten code of ethics determines how a participant must relate to others in the bureaucracy. This code is constantly evolving through changes in the written rules, personnel, and the general environment.[1]

Thus, Morton Halperin sets out admirably the basis on which a comparison of the two defence organisation will be attempted.

The style of defence policymaking in the two countries is very different. In the United Kingdom, Defence by Discussion should, if it is successful, involve resource allocation problems being examined by the Services on neutral ground for at least part of the time, with the Chiefs of Staff Committee playing a vital part in the final decision. In the United States, Defence by Bargaining is likely to prevail unless a strong Secretary of Defense, supported by his President, seeks to impose decisions about resource allocation on the Services. In the United States, however, the broad guidelines of strategy, and, on occasion, the broad allocation of resources will be laid down under the President's general authority by the National Security Council and its staff, and at one remove by the Office of Management and Budget; that is, by agencies outside the Department of Defense. This participation in defence policymaking by those outside the defence organisation is more marked in the United States than in the United Kingdom.

To discover why the status of the Service departments and therefore the methods of making decisions about defence resources differ, one must study the "rules of the game," and this is best done under headings similar to those mentioned by Morton Halperin in the preceding quotation. This chapter will examine the organisation of the executive branch of the government, and this organisation will be related in the following chapter to the power of the legislature to affect defence policy in general and resource allocation in particular. The next chapter will consider the role of those, other than legislators, outside the defence bureaucracy. These comparisons are being made not to find whether one system is better than the other, but to see, if possible, why adversary relationships between the Services have been more strongly marked in the United States than in the United Kingdom.

THE CHIEF EXECUTIVE

Clearly, the constitutional position of the chief executive (whether one person or a group of people) and the limitations on his power by other centres of power and authority in the state will have a significant effect on matters relating to defence. By tradition, and with good reason, the defence of the realm has been considered in both the United Kingdom and the United States to be of special concern to the chief executive, and undoubtedly this tradition will continue in the future. The supreme authority in the executive in the United Kingdom lies with the cabinet. There is no advantage for the present enquiry in taking sides in the debate on whether the United Kingdom has cabinet or prime ministerial government. In any case, the major issues of defence policy would be brought before the cabinet itself or a cabinet committee, of which the Prime Minister is chairman.

Although the Secretary of State for Defence would be expected to bring major issues forward, the cabinet is not regarded as, or designed to be, a forum in which judgment can be delivered on conflicting interests or arguments that are wholly within the area of responsibility of one of its members. The minister responsible for defence would therefore be expected to propose a broad allocation of expenditure among the Armed Services. A minister may find his proposals rejected, or he might be asked to modify them, but his colleagues in the cabinet are not, in general, briefed to decide upon controversial issues within another ministry, and do not wish to sit in judgment on contending factions that should owe allegiance to another minister. Each minister wishes to be master in his own house; he opposes interference in his own and refrains from interfering in another's ministry.[2] The fact that the Chief of the Defence Staff (CDS), (and in the past all the Chiefs of Staff) may attend cabinet (and cabinet committee) meetings as an adviser should not be taken as an indication that the cabinet welcomes inter-Service partisan debate at its meetings. A notable example in the defence field occurred when Mr. Healey, as part of a series of major decisions on defence expenditure, rejected proposals to build further aircraft carriers for the Royal Navy. This decision involved eventually phasing out all aircraft carriers in service, and the minister responsible for the Royal Navy asked permission to present arguments against such a serious step to the cabinet in person. Mr. Healey refused him this permission.[3]

The Secretary of State for Defence is, then, subject to the continuing support of his cabinet colleagues, completely in charge of defence business, and able to speak in Parliament with the full authority of the government on all defence matters. He can, moreover, present his proposals for defence expenditure, secure in the knowledge that the government majority in the legislature will ensure that they are agreed without change. Even if no overall government majority exists, the acceptance by Parliament of proposals on defence expenditure would be treated as a matter of confidence, so that the rejection of them would entail the dissolution of Parliament and a general election. There is, therefore, little temptation for institutions within the executive, such as the Armed Services, to bypass the correct channels of authority if, in their view, their proper requirements for resources are not being met. They have much to lose by doing so and are likely to gain more by working within the system. "In Britain," as Laurence Martin writes, "the ultimate objective of an attempt to revise a matter of broad policy must be to change the mind of the cabinet."[4]

In the United States the rules are different. The President, both as commander in chief of the armed forces, and as chief executive, has a special responsibility for defence. He himself presents proposals on defence expenditure to the legislature as part of his budget, and thus far, it could be argued, there is a close parallel with the United Kingdom—in both cases defence expenditure proposals are presented to the legislature with the authority of the chief executive, in the one case the cabinet, and in the other the President. But here the similarity ends. "The Founding Fathers," as Richard Hofstadter writes, believed that "a properly designed state would check interest with interest, class with class, faction with faction, and one branch of government with another, in a harmonious system of mutual frustration."[5] Although the President is responsible for proposing defence expenditure, only Congress has the power to approve expenditure for this purpose, and the President cannot command an automatic majority in Congress.

The same is also true of legislation, and the effects of these significant differences in the constitutional rules of the game in the two countries will have to be examined in a number of contexts. It is important now, however, to note that in the United States the power of the executive over its subordinate organisations is not absolute and to draw some conclusions from this. There must clearly be a temptation for those agencies in the US government that are disappointed with their budget allocations to make a separate approach to Congress to reopen the argument. Whether these attempts are usually successful is not the point; the fact that in the past the Services have appealed directly to Congress serves to maintain the adversary relationships among the Services and to put a premium on the need to maintain their independence from one another.

The Services have little to gain from any sacrifice of their freedom to lobby if they always have the chance of appeal to a power outside the executive. The expression "end run" from American football may or may not be appropriate to describe the manoeuvres by which Congress may reallocate resources among the Services (the next chapter will consider the extent to which this does happen), but it is important to note that genuine differences of opinion among the Services on matters of major strategy may quite properly come to the attention of Congress through consitutional procedures, resulting in an erosion of the power of the executive. General Taylor's experience as Chief of Staff for the Army, when he profoundly disagreed with the New Look Strategy of the Eisenhower administration, is a case in point:

> The open testimony of the Chiefs of Staff before the Johnson subcommittee had a country-wide impact. Along with their testimony released from the closed hearings before other congressional committees, it revealed for the first time the extent of the schism within the Joint Chiefs of Staff and the division of their views on Massive Retaliation and related matters of strategy. This revelation profoundly disturbed many members of Congress, as well as thoughtful citizens generally. This healthy state of alarm had the benefit of creating a climate favorable to a demand for the reappraisal of strategic needs which had become so necessary.[6]

THE DEFENCE SECRETARY

Similar considerations affect the position of the Secretary of Defense in the United States in comparison with his counterpart in the United Kingdom, whose authority over the Service departments is not impeded or restricted by any other organ of government, provided, of course, he has the support of his cabinet colleagues. In the United Kingdom, he is traditionally a relatively major political figure within the party in power, and is likely to carry great weight in the cabinet when speaking on defence matters. As has already been noted, the Chief of the Defence Staff may attend meetings of cabinet ministers, and Service advice will therefore be directly available to ministers before major decisions are taken. But under the rules of the game this is the limit to which Service advice on the allocation of defence resources can go, which is not to say that defence is exempted from the annual battle in Whitehall among the spending departments. Indeed, the contrary is the case; the allocation of funds to defence is, and must be, a matter for argument at many levels within the system, and as a result the Treasury could well have strong views on the proposed allocation of the budget among the three Services. But it is important to stress that these views, if pressed by the Chancellor of the Exchequer, would finally be put to the Secretary of State himself, not to junior ministers or others responsible for particular Services, and still less to the professional heads of the Services themselves; and lobbying in the reverse direction is an equally unlikely feature of the Whitehall scene. However the situation is analysed or examined, the focus of bureaucratic politics and inter-Service argument in the United Kingdom is seen to be the Secretary of State for Defence himself. It is through him that issues will be put to the cabinet and through him that decisions will be conveyed to the Services.

Following the 1947 defence reorganisation in the United States, there were evidently some who thought that the newly created Secretary of Defense should operate in the same way as the Secretary of State for Defence. Mr. Truman wrote: "Secretary of Defense Forrestal had for some time been advocating our using the British cabinet system as a model in the operation of the government. There is much to this idea—in some ways a cabinet government is more efficient—but under the British system there is a group responsibility of the cabinet. Under our system the responsibility rests on one man—the President. To change, we would have to change our Constitution."[7] This quotation very clearly states the position in the United States, and one must conclude that the power and authority of the US Secretary of Defense over the US Armed Services must to some extent at any rate be weakened by the fact that he is in essence an adviser to the President, and not as in the United Kingdom, a part of what S. E. Finer calls the "collective presidency of the cabinet."[8]

It may be argued that a Secretary of Defense who has the complete confidence of his President would not suffer under such a handicap and would exercise complete control over the Services. It is, however, doubtful whether a complete identity of view over all defence problems could long endure; even the consistent support that Presidents Kennedy and Johnson gave to Mr. McNamara in defence matters was not sufficient, for example, to prevent the President acting contrary to Mr. McNamara's advice on the ABM problem. But even if such perfect harmony did exist, the Services would not be tempted to forfeit any of their independence because such identity of view would not be likely to survive a change of President or Secretary of Defense.

The power and authority of the Secretary of Defense over resource allocation is further weakened in comparison with his UK counterpart by two government agencies, both responsible directly to the President and both directly concerned with defence. The National Security Council (NSC) has been in existence since the 1947 reorganisation of the Defense Department, but the number and influence of staff allocated to it was increased by President Nixon in 1969. Presidents have used the council to widen the area of debate when they were at odds with their Secretaries of Defense in bilateral discussions. Thus, President Johnson referred the ABM question to the council when the Secretary of Defense opposed his point of view.[9] It is not difficult to imagine a President making a similar move in the future if he was doubtful about the views of the Secretary of Defense on an inter-Service problem.

The influence and potential power of the NSC staff, however, are even greater than is implied by the foregoing. In 1972, the Defense Program Review Committee (DPRC) of the council was instituted with supporting staff. The committee was, as the name implies, to advise the President and the National Security Council, not only on the total of the Defense Budget, but also on which of the major defence projects should be included in it. The opportunity that confers upon a President to take major resource allocation decisions away from the Secretary of Defense has not, by all accounts, been frequently used; but the opportunity is there, and recent major decisions, such as the cancellation and then the reintroduction of the B1 bomber, have clearly been made by the President himself. This must surely contribute to the desire of the Service departments to remain independent and able to fight their case in whatever forum the final decision is going to be made.

The Office of Management and Budget (OMB) has the potential to fulfill the same function for the President. Some of the OMB staff are housed in the same building as the Department of Defense, and are concerned exclusively with the defence budget.[10] Their influence on the final allocation is powerful, since the staffs of the Office of Management and Budget and the Office of the Secretary of Defense (OSD) jointly review the detailed spending plans of the Services. Moreover, when the Secretary of Defense submits his final budget proposals to the President, the Office of Management and Budget submits separate findings and recommendations on issues that remain in dispute between the OSD and the OMB staffs.

Although the legal right of individual JCS members to appeal to the President both from an adverse vote of the Joint Chiefs of Staff and an adverse decision of the Secretary of Defense has been discontinued, the Services tend to regard the President himself as the proper source from which any necessary but unpalatable decisions should come. "The President," writes Lawrence Legere, "is accepted as a member of the military family in a way that no Secretary of Defense has yet been able to manage. As he reinforces that perception, he will find senior military leaders increasingly content to report back to their constituencies that the President heard them through, expressed his understanding, but had to adduce overriding considerations of a broadly political nature."[11]

The ability of the Secretary of Defense to control the Service departments is to a significant extent weakened by the President's position as head of the Armed Services and by the President's ability to intervene in the major decisions about resource allocation in the Defense Department. Similarly, the power of the President himself is limited by the power the Constitution gives to Congress to intervene in the making of defence policy. The rules of the US game, so far as the executive is concerned, therefore encourage an independence of attitude and action by the US Armed Services, both individually and collectively, which is not open to their counterparts in the United Kingdom.

So far, however, the examples mentioned have related to decisions about defence expenditure. This emphasis has not been unreasonable, because resource allocation among the Services is the main area of study. But it should not be forgotten that Congress also has legislative powers, and can use these powers to maintain the independence of the three Services, which is such a notable feature of American defence policymaking. According to Morton Halperin, "both President Truman and President Eisenhower carried on extensive negotiations with the military in the recognition that they were unlikely to be able to get any reorganisation plan through the Congress which did not have military support."[12] In amplification of this point, he quotes President Eisenhower's advice to President Kennedy about reorganising the Department of Defense, "that the present organisation had during the past eight years been brought about by patient study and long, drawn-out negotiations with the Congress and the Armed Services."[13] No better illustration of the effect of the separation of powers upon defence policymaking can be found. In this field, as in others, the power of the President is confronted by the power of Congress, and it is now clearly necessary to consider the power of the legislature over defence policy in both countries.

CONCLUSION

In Britain, the executive can normally command an automatic majority in Parliament, which therefore has no veto on defence policy. In the United States, however, despite their powers to initiate policy and appoint their nominees to carry it out, neither the President nor his Secretary of Defense have the last word on defence resource allocation or defence organisation. Congress must approve both before they can come into effect. If a Service is dissatisfied with the President's decision in either area, it can find ways of bringing this disquiet to the notice of Congress. The next chapter discusses what Congress can do about this dissatisfaction.

Chapter Six
Structure: The Legislature

UNITED KINGDOM

"The House of Commons," as S. E. Finer remarks, "is not a true legislature but an extension of the executive,"[1] and is therefore unlikely to be able to take any initiatives in the formulation of defence policy by the exercise of its own powers. If policy is to be made or changed, then the legislature may act as a sounding board or as a leader of public opinion. This topic will be discussed in the following chapter since it properly forms part of the process of changing the mind of the cabinet, referred to in the previous chapter.

It may be argued that the power of Parliament to question ministers through the traditional process of parliamentary questions is an effective method of control over the executive. This is not so. Opposition members of parliament are not supported either by research facilities or the investigative powers of the US senator or congressman. The main function of parliamentary questions, and of arrangements for debate on subjects chosen by the opposition, is to provide opportunity for criticism rather than investigation. A Select Committee on Procedure in 1969 said, "Though it is the business of the government to govern, it is also their business to give a running account of their stewardship to the House of Commons."[2]

The main parliamentary committees concerned with defence are the Public Accounts Committee and the House of Commons Defence Committee. Both committees have the power to "call for persons and papers," and the appearance of senior Service officers and civil servants before them is a regular occurrence. But in neither case do these committees have power to change government policy. The first committee, as its names implies, is confined to examining the propriety of past expenditure and cannot have great influence on future policy. The terms of reference of the Defence Committee are certainly wider, and it may examine major areas of expenditure and criticise the policy giving rise to that expenditure. But the influence of the Defence Committee on future policy can only, at best, be indirect, and officials who appear before it are only required to explain government policy and not to expound their own views, or those of their Service if these views happen to differ from the stated policy of the government.

It is therefore unlikely that a parliamentary committee would be able to open a major debate on defence policy similar to that started in the United States on the New Look Strategy by the evidence of General Taylor and others in the 1950s. If such a debate were to happen, it would be because the government supporters on the Defence Committee had decided that the national interest was so great thay they must threaten to withhold support from the government and risk its falling rather than allow a particular aspect of defence policy to remain unchallenged and unchanged. If parliamentary select committees are in the future able to force major changes in government policy in this way, a new and striking change in the existing system will have evolved. Until a parliamentary committee achieves this power, one would expect governments to be influenced more by debate amongst their own supporters than by debate in the legislature itself or its subordinate committees. This point is discussed at more length at the end of this chapter.

The rights of the legislature in the United Kingdom, therefore, do not include the power to force changes in defence policy on the executive, provided the executive retains the support of a majority in the House of Commons. "When," Michael Howard writes, "as in Great Britain the executive can command an automatic legislative majority, the defeated or disgruntled parties are prevented from reopening a 'chose jugeé' and throwing everything into confusion."[3] Clearly, in these circumstances the Armed Services are not likely to have the opportunity or the desire individually or collectively to force changes in government policy by direct appeal to the legislature.

UNITED STATES

The previous chapter examined the extent to which the power of the United States executive over defence policy was inhibited by the power of the legislature. Now the opposite side of the coin must be inspected to try to determine the answer to two questions: Does the legislature have a significant influence on defence policy? and Does the exercise of power by the legislature in any way foster the independence of and the adversary relationships among the Services? It is, of course, possible that the answer to the second question might be yes, even if the answer to the first was no.

The rivalry between the President and Congress is built into the Constitution, which gives Congress two strong weapons to use to check presidential power. Congress can delay or refuse to enact bills submitted by the President, and it can cut or change the appropriations of money requested by the President. A particularly galling example is given by a former Director of the Bureau of the Budget:

> A few years ago agreement was reached between the Bureau and the Defense Department on closing two large military hospitals, one in Arkansas and the other in Massachusetts, that were no longer needed. New adjacent facilities were quite adequate. However, the interests affected were successful in blocking this economy move by getting a directive written into an appropriations bill covering many billions of dollars, stating that none of these funds could be used if either of these two hospitals were closed down. I could give a number of similar examples.[4]

This example at least shows the power of Congress over appropriation of funds, but this power is not necessarily always used for such parochial interests. In 1960, Samuel Huntington could write:

> After World War II, except when confronted by similar competing programs, Congress never vetoed directly a major strategic program or force-level recommendation, or a major weapons system proposed by the Administration. Nor did the Congress ever achieve this result, with one partial exception (the Navy's second nuclear carrier), through the failure to appropriate funds recommended by the Executive.... Almost regularly, of course, Congress reduced the total request, but it virtually never did this in a manner which seriously affected a major strategic program.[5]

It is doubtful whether the same statement could now be made with such assurance.[6] Congress took an active part in the proposals for extensive ABM deployments. Moreover, Congress has in the past refused to sanction expenditure on fast deployment logistic ships for the Navy and, at an earlier stage in the appropriations process, withheld agreement to the Main Battle Tank and the Cheyenne Helicopter. Finally, congressional concern with the production and deployment of the MX missile in 1980–82 shows the extent to which strategic policy may be altered by the intervention of Congress.

However, it is not necessary to prove or disprove Professor Huntington's statement to answer the question relating to congressional influence on US defence policy. In the light of the historical examples referred to above, it must be accepted that Congress has a significant influence on defence policy in general and weapons programmes in particular, whether or not it has the last word. This influence must surely deter an administration from making proposals that are likely to encounter strong opposition in Congress; and the Services will certainly wish to retain an independent voice in favour of those projects that the administration does put forward. Many senior military officers consider that the vital interests of their own Service are best protected by maintaining the good standing of their Service with Congress.

One important point needs to be made before considering the second question. Members of Congress do not feel themselves well-equipped to be responsible for national security. They are normally content to leave the initiative on defence policy to the executive. Moreover, as L. A. Dexter pointed out, "instances where Congress has appeared to concern itself with overall military policy seem generally to fall into one of the following categories: (i) those where Congress feels it is able to judge between clamoring claimants—usually different military services—and give one or other of them a larger slice of the available pie; and, (ii) where Congressmen are concerned with some local situation, usually an employment situation."[7] To these remarks, one should perhaps now add, in light of the 1982 MX debates, that Congress may well intervene far more strongly when decisions are being taken about basing nuclear weapons in the United States.

Nevertheless, whether or not Congress does have a decisive say in making defence policy, the role of Congress has undoubtedly been important in continuing the Services' adversary relationship. The proviso in the quotation from Samuel Huntington given earlier in this chapter, "except when confronted by similar competing programs," is significant in this context. Their natural and proper instinct for economy will clearly encourage senators and congressmen to probe into areas where the efforts of the Services appear to compete and overlap.

Congressional enquiries are bound to stimulate competition between the Services, each of which will be tempted in these situations both to overstate the case and to make extreme demands on the assumption that compromises will be forced on them. It is true that there has been some restriction in the freedom which Service officers enjoyed under the Truman administration, and previously, to volunteer the information before congressional committees that they disagreed with proposals put forward by the administration. Thus, in the 1960s Mr. McNamara was able to "impose a much more restrictive rule: that the military reveal differences only if pressed, and then, in admitting the disagreement give the administration's side of the case as well."[8] But this change can surely do little to lessen the need for the Services to maintain their independence to argue their case before Congress. "Each military service," as Laurence Radway writes, "has at some time appealed to Congress to restore budgets cut by the Secretary of Defense. Admiral Rickover appealed to Congress when he believed that the Navy was neglecting the atomic submarine program;

Air Force General Le May appealed when he felt that the test ban treaty endangered national security."[9]

Here, it is only necessary to note that in appealing from the executive to the legislature the Services are making proper use of the Constitution based on the concept of the separation of powers, and to quote Laurence Radway again: "Members of Congress in their turn are shrewd enough to sense that they may be able to enhance their own influence by increasing disunity in the bureaucracy. Their obvious gambit is to try to divide and rule by limiting the supervisory authority of superiors (hence outcries against both a 'Prussian' general staff and a civilian 'Czar' in the Pentagon), by vesting statutory authority and funds directly in subordinates, and by encouraging or tempting the latter to appeal decisions made by their superiors."[10]

Hitherto, the discussion of the relationship between Congress and the Services has concentrated on the effects of the congressional powers of appropriation, but as just indicated, Congress has reasons of its own for wishing to see the Services retain a measure of independence. One of the main reasons is that Congress wishes to preserve the right to question representatives of the Armed Services and will use its legislative powers to do so. These powers must now be considered.

Demetrios Caraley writes in his study of the unification of the US Armed Services: "The two chief formal methods of exercising congressional control over the executive branch agencies are through the appropriations process and through statutory determination of their organisational structure and programs."[11] As Caraley's study shows, Congress is not reluctant to exercise its power over the defence organisation. During the 1946 and 1947 debates on unification, Congress worked to produce a defence organisation that gave greater independence to the Service departments than was envisaged in the President's original proposals. This objective involved diminishing the authority of the central defence organisation, with the result that, as Caraley explains, a "military structure with separate or relatively autonomous military departments, each with its own set of spokesmen appearing before Congress, could provide the legislators with more than a single point of view on military matters and thus give them some freedom of action in formulating policy."[12]

Another illustration of the use of these powers to achieve this end has already been noted in chapter 5. Both President Truman and President Eisenhower had in effect to negotiate with the Armed Services and with Congress over the extent to which the unification of the Services should proceed. Moreover, as Morton Halperin remarks, "Congressmen often see it as their duty to protect the permanent bureaucracy against encroachments by the President and cabinet officers."[13] He goes on to instance the occasion when President Eisenhower's Secretary of Defense appeared before the relevant House committee to testify in favour of the reorganisation plan that the President himself had sent to Congress. Mr. McElroy did not appear to be so much in favour of the bill as the President and gave the impression that some concession on the powers of the Secretary of Defense to control the Armed Services could be considered. The chairman of the committee seized on this point, and President Eisenhower had to publicly overrule his own Secretary of Defense and send word to Congress that no further concession would be made in the bill before Congress.

More recent events, such as the controversy over the Vietnam war, the congressional reluctance to sanction further overseas commitments (for example in Angola), and the MX debate, might be considered to invalidate the view that members of Congress do not consider themselves defence experts and leave the initiative to the executive. Further consideration shows, however, that Congress is taking a stand on major issues of foreign policy or nuclear strategy which are, in some sense at least, peace or war issues rather than detailed matters of resource allocation among the Services. It is still true to say that on these latter issues members of Congress do not consider that they have the detailed and expert knowledge that would allow them to take the initiative; but as in the past, they will, in the Armed Services and Appropriations Committees, judge competing service claimants for defence funds. If in the future Congress intervenes more decisively in decisions about strategic nuclear weapons, then this intervention will provide another disincentive to the Services to reach agreement on issues of major concern to them before each has assessed the strength of its support in Congress.

THE PARTY SYSTEM IN THE UNITED KINGDOM AND IN THE UNITED STATES

Clearly, no discussion of the role of the legislature in defence policy-making can ignore the system of political parties in each country. But as these parties have noticeable effects on the extent and level of public debate on both sides of the Atlantic, it seems best to treat the role of the party system separately from the role of the legislature as such, thereby linking this chapter and the next.

As far as the United Kingdom is concerned, it might be thought that there was little to add. The fact that the executive can command an automatic majority in the legislature would seem to leave no role for party politics in the formulation of defence policy. But there is another side to this assumption. It is true that government supporters in the House of Commons risk their seats by opposing government measures because a defeat could well entail a dissolution of Parliament; but it is equally true that the government risks defeat and therefore the dissolution of Parliament if it flouts the wishes of its supporters. Both sides have some power over the other and back benchers are not always docile lobby fodder.

This has led Kenneth Waltz to make an extremely interesting and persuasive comparison between the formulation of foreign (and defence) policy in the United Kingdom and the United States.[14] He stresses that the important policy debates in the United Kingdom occur within the government (and opposition) parties, whereas in the United States these debates occur in a wider forum either in Congress or in the nation as a whole.

For the purpose of this study, one need not argue, as Professor Waltz seems to do, that the only debates in Britain influencing present and future government policy are those conducted either within the political party in power or within the party that may gain power at the next election, although it is certainly a persuasive theory in the light of the Labour party debates in 1974–75 on membership in the European Economic Community. But whatever the validity of this general proposition, it is correct to state that, to the extent to which it is true, there are two serious impediments to the intervention of senior officers and defence officials in such debates. First, these debates are by their nature likely to be confined to committed members of the political party concerned, and second, the ban on senior public servants engaging in political activities is almost certain to deter public intervention by the Services in such discussions.

There is, as Professor Waltz argues, no obvious equivalent in the United States to the intraparty debate in the United Kingdom. The President cannot command an automatic majority in the Congress, and one would not therefore expect to find instances of a government making considerable concessions to a minority of its own supporters in order to secure their assent to passage of some proposal through the legislature. A US government is more likely to seek support from both political parties to ensure the passage of their proposals through Congress, and this clearly involves a public and interparty debate. However, before each presidential election, something like the intraparty debate in the United Kingdom takes place in the United States as both parties debate and prepare the policies that will form their presidential candidates' platforms.

As Demetrios Caraley points out, congressional party leaders, unlike their counterparts in the British House of Commons, cannot automatically create majorities in Congress for proposals they endorse.[15] The history of the President's proposals on defence organisation in 1946 illustrates this point. Even though the original proposal on defence reorganisation received high priority from President Truman in 1946, the Democratic leadership took no overt action to support it. Their support was exercised in less obvious ways. As Caraley remarks, "the party leaders. . .through their influence over committee makeup, the referral of bills, the legislative schedule, and the parliamentary situation generally, were able to facilitate or hinder the development and adoption of different kinds of committee recommendation on unification." This support is in striking contrast to the two or three line whips (instructions on whether to vote for or against proposals being debated) issued to government supporters when major defence proposals are considered in the British Parliament.

Interestingly enough, when the President's proposals were first introduced in 1946 they were not passed by Congress. They were passed in 1947 when the debate in Congress was resumed, but by that time significant changes had been secured by those opposed to the complete unification of the Services. The looser structure of political parties in the United States must therefore, if past experience is any guide, persuade Service leaders to continue the fight against a government decision in the hope of securing sufficient congressional support to persuade the President to compromise or even abandon his proposals.

SPECIAL INTERESTS AND LOBBY GROUPS

After considering the members of Congress both as a part of the legislature and as members of a political party, it may be useful to discuss briefly another set of pressures with which they will be faced. As has often been pointed out,[16] the separation of powers attracts pressure group activity for a number of reasons, and this pressure is exerted on the individual member of Congress who is, of course, particularly susceptible to regional or local pressures from the area he represents. It would not be thought unusual or wrong for either senators or congressmen to argue for the interests of their state or district even if those interests appeared to the majority to be contrary to the national interest. Thus, congressional representatives of areas likely to benefit from a major weapon purchase might well feel that they owed it to their constituents to try to obtain the contract for their district or state despite doubts about the overall benefit to national defence.

The Service concerned can expect to find willing allies in Congress in any fight to secure approval of a major weapons programme, and the existence of this support is likely to be known both within the executive and in Congress, an example is the saga of the B1 bomber discussed in the next chapter. The restrictions that party discipline imposes on British members of Parliament make it unlikely that they would go to the same lengths as their counterparts in the United States to advance their constituents' interests.

In this context, therefore, the three Services and other groups or interests within the executive can be seen as a particular form of special interest able to deploy some of the pressures open to the more well-known lobby groups. Caraley describes how some of these pressures were used in the 1946–47 debates on defence organisation and later goes on to remark: "The rules of the game generally, and the norms of Congress in particular, protect independence and freedom of expression within subordinate parts of the executive branch. . . ." An attempt to curb freedom of expression within the executive branch is very readily interpreted as an attack on congressional authority.[17]

Finally, it should be noted that the impact of the criticisms of US defence organisation that General Jones made in 1982 was significantly increased when Congressman Richard White, Chairman of the Investigations Subcommittee of the House Armed Services Committee, called hearings of his subcommittee and subsequently put forward a bill to rectify some of the defects pointed out by General Jones. Individual members of Congress are dedicated to such esoteric subjects as defence organisation because those who chair or are members of the relevant committees feel a personal sense of responsibility for the areas of government activity covered by their committees. This attitude would not come naturally to back-bench members of the British Parliament. This sense of shared responsibility between executive and legislature is one of the beneficial aspects of the doctrine of the separation of powers.

CONCLUSION

It seems a fair conclusion, therefore, that the nature of the US legislature, the system of party politics, and the pressures on individual members of Congress are all such as to encourage rather than discourage the independence of the Services, thereby contributing to the adversary relationship between them. In the United Kingdom, those within the executive who wish to change either existing government policy or even a single government decision know that they must change the mind of the cabinet, and neither the forum of Parliament nor a party meeting is an appropriate place for a Service officer or civil servant to do that. In contrast, members of the US armed forces owe their freedom to speak in public against current defence policy to the powers of Congress to withhold defence expenditure and to veto major changes in defence organisation.

Chapter Seven

The Influence of Outsiders on Inter-Service Rivalry

In a very real sense the preceding chapter has set the scene for, and prescribed the limits of, a discussion of the effect of outside influences on inter-Service rivalry. In the United Kingdom, public discussion of a defence question must, if it is to be effective, influence the cabinet either directly or through the medium of intraparty discussion among government supporters in the legislature. If, therefore, this study devotes less attention than expected to the role of the press or the influence of elite groups, it is because the aim is not to assess the effect of various sectors of public opinion on the formulation of defence policy; instead, it is to see whether the style of public debate about defence issues is likely to encourage the Services to air their differences in public as a means of influencing defence policy and the allocation of defence resources.

In the United States, influence on defence policy formulation is spread more widely than in the United Kingdom. Both the executive and the legislature influence policy, and proponents of alternatives to the current defence policy will seek to carry on the argument both inside and outside government. Issues on which the Services differ strongly are therefore almost certain to receive a public airing.

The remarks in this chapter apply to the range of issues in defence policy on which the Services could take different sides. They cannot necessarily be applied to the wider range of public issues on which debates are held, and political elections fought, in a democratic society. Public opinion overtly and freely expressed is the essential basis of the liberal democratic form of government and as S. E. Finer emphasises,[1] such governments are both derived from public opinion and accountable to it. However, the major issues dividing political parties in the United Kingdom and the United States are not ones on which by tradition the Services themselves are willing to take an open stand, because apart from other considerations the doctrine of civilian supremacy over the armed forces is well established in both countries. This chapter can therefore confine itself to issues of defence policy involving allocation of resources to each of the Services which, though important, are not likely to be the subject of fierce partisan controversy at election time.

UNITED KINGDOM

The reluctance of British Service officers (and civil servants as well) to engage in public debate during the second half of the present century is well known.[2] Clearly, however, pronounced and prolonged alarm at the likely consequence of a government's decisions on defence policy may diminish the reluctance of serving officers to participate in a debate in which retired Service officers, particularly those who are members of Parliament, will have no doubt already joined. In his review of the Sandys era,[3] Laurence Martin mentions an instance of Service participation in the debate on the Sandys doctrine, which is particularly interesting because the comparison between it and General Maxwell Taylor's intervention in the debate in the United States on the New Look strategy is revealing.

The salient features of the incident can be briefly summarised. Lieutenant General Sir John Cowley, Master-General of the Ordnance and Controller of Munitions, Ministry of Supply, lectured at the Royal United Service Institute on 4 November 1959. He condemned reliance on nuclear weapons to deter war and harshly criticised the neglect of conventional forces. He further pointed out that he was on active service, and this implied that his speech had been approved by the Secretary of State for War. His open criticism of stated government policy brought a swift reaction. It was announced in the House of Commons on 11 November[4] that in the future the speeches of senior officers would have to be cleared by the Ministry of Defence. It is equally illuminating that the opposition endorsed this decision and thus made it clear that there was to be no open and independent role for the Services in any public debate on defence policy, whichever party was in power. In contrast, the US Congress is likely to seek to protect those within the bureaucracy who criticise existing policy.

The attitude of the British press toward the Services is hard to define. Comment in the more serious newspapers on the 1982 changes in defence organisation appeared to treat inter-Service rivalry as a matter of fact requiring neither explanation not stern condemnation. In the more popular press there seems to be an element of affectionate but almost contemptuous tolerance for this feature of defence policymaking. The cartoonist David Low used to illustrate military prejudice by Colonel Blimp, a comic elderly buffer in a Turkish bath, and in a more recent cartoon by "Jak" of the London *Evening Standard* the office of the Defence Planning Staff has come to resemble a schoolroom taken over for battle by rowdy school boys.

The government now follows a somewhat more liberal policy regarding the participation by serving officers and officials in a public discussion of defence problems. Under the so called Chatham House Rules, Service officers and civil servants may speak unattributively at conferences run by certain universities and learned institutions. This policy change is in keeping with the move toward a greater openness in the work of government as a whole in the United Kingdom. The change entails providing the fullest possible explanation of the reasons for policies the government has adopted, thereby creating a better understanding of the way in which the government machine actually works.

But this change of policy is more a change of emphasis than a change of heart. Open government is not intended to cover public discussions by officials and serving officers of defence policies still being formulated; nor should they address subjects that are likely to be matters of controversy between political parties. Their participation must neither embarrass the government nor raise doubts as to the impartiality of the Armed Services or the civil service. The use in official statements and instructions of the word "impartiality" is illuminating to American readers. They will no doubt feel that much of the edge will be taken off a public debate when the critic of defence policy cannot, unless he is a member of Parliament and subsequently a minister of the Crown, expect that he himself will implement the new policy he advocates, but must see it put into effect by impartial government servants who will not have been involved directly in the debate. At least some of the fire and enthusiasm of the "Best and Brightest" of the Kennedy era must have been due to a natural and proper ambition on their part to become decisionmakers themselves.

UNITED STATES

When considering the role and effects of public opinion in the United States, one must bear in mind the demands and pressures the executive and the legislature frequently make upon the Services to speak with a single-Service rather than a defence voice. The point now at issue is whether debate in the public arena makes the same or similar demands. There is a distinction, even if it is a fine one, between debate in the legislature where both parties are seeking to influence a vote, and thus invoke legislative power, and the broader more free-ranging public discussions of defence and foreign policy issues that take place outside Congress. The outcome of the latter must affect the thinking of those in the executive or the legislature before it can influence actions.

The first example of public debate to be considered, in most respects, belies the name. In 1954, the Eisenhower administration wanted, or appeared to want, a congressional resolution to permit the President to use air and naval power in Indochina to assist the French garrison besieged at Dienbienphu. This was an issue on which the executive, and even more important for the present study, the Joint Chiefs of Staff, were divided. The President himself was evidently lukewarm,[5] but Mr. Dulles, Secretary of State, and Admiral Radford, Chairman of the Joint Chiefs of Staff, were both in favour. A meeting was arranged on 3 April 1954, between Mr. Dulles, Admiral Radford, and the congressional leadership, including Senators Knowland and Johnson.

The meeting started with a forceful presentation by Admiral Radford in favour of an air strike on the forces besieging Dienbienphu; but questioning by Senator Johnson elicited the fact that other members of the Joint Chiefs of Staff were opposed to this course of action, and that the United States did not have the support of Britain or any other allies except France. As a result, the Democratic leadership in Congress refused its support for the proposal, and an acrimonious debate took place in Congress some days later. If, as David Halberstam suggests, President Eisenhower himself had strong reservations about military intervention, then clearly "the President had once again used the Congress as a sounding board and had quickly sensed deep reservations."[6] Public opinion as much as the floor of Congress was the bar at which this issue was decided, and the absence of Service unanimity was a crucial argument in rejecting the proposal for military intervention.

The issue raised in that example was literally peace or war and may not seem relevant to issues of resource allocation with which this study is mainly concerned. But, if the Services are encouraged to take an independent stand on such vital national issues, they will certainly wish to seek the same privilege when other issues vital to their continued existence are raised. It is also admittedly a curious example of public debate since the public was not directly involved in it. But President Eisenhower used the meeting with congressional leaders as an indication of what a public debate would be like if it took place, and if, in consequence, the differing views of the Service leaders were displayed in public.

However, an essential ingredient in a public debate is the power of press, radio, and television to inform, to educate, and to influence the public on defence and foreign policy issues. This power is a serious responsibility when one considers that the public is likely to be far less well informed on these matters than on domestic issues. "The American System," as Laurence Radway writes,[7] "provides the press with many clear windows and open doors. It presumes that public policy is public property and that public servants ought to be available to their masters." Be that as it may, one can detect an element of watchfulness, almost hostility, in the American press toward the Services and especially toward the demands of the defence budget. There is a sharper tone to the American press, which contrasts with the relative tolerance of the British press. Again cartoons seem to bear out this view. A survey of over twenty years of US political cartoons has failed to find one matching the attitude of "Jak," mentioned above, but many reveal press hostility toward large military budgets. It is clear that the American press is well aware of inter-Service rivalry and numerous examples could be given where disagreements between the Services have been probed by the press, often after an approach by one of the Services engaged in the controversy.

Although Service officers have been reprimanded for over-zealous and public advocacy of the Service case, in general the press is used, or uses its Service sources, with some discretion.[8] Nevertheless, the relative openness with which US Service officers and civil servants will provide information and comment is in marked contrast to their opposite numbers in the United Kingdom. In consequence, it is not difficult during inter-Service controversy for a journalist to collect sufficient material for a reasonably accurate article quoting Pentagon sources. The ability of the Services to speak independently, and if necessary anonymously, to the press seems to be an important if not essential part of the US thesis that public policy is public property, and to the extent that this freedom is maintained, the independence of the Services is also buttressed.

Another good example of public debate relates to the change in US strategy in the early 1960s when the Eisenhower New Look strategy was converted to one of flexible response across the whole spectrum of war. As Seyom Brown writes:

> Kennedy's general premises about the nation's military requirements were well developed before he assumed the Presidency and were very much the conventional wisdom among the Democrats involved in foreign policy matters. But the premises themselves were not the product of partisan politics however they may have been invoked to that effect. They were the product of a number of strains of strategic thought that had now converged: the ideas generated by Paul Nitze and the Policy Planning Council in NSC–68, the 1950 document reflecting on the military planning implications of the soon-to-come Soviet intercontinental nuclear capability; the Air Force-RAND Corporation arguments for a survivable ("invulnerable") strategic retaliatory force (also favored by the Navy as the major rationale for the Polaris submarine-fired missile); the doctrine of "flexible response" put forward within the Eisenhower administration by Army Chiefs of Staff Matthew Ridgway and Maxwell Taylor in opposition to the strategic monism of Secretary of State Dulles and Admiral Radford; the analysis of the possibilities for limited war in the thermonuclear age by scholars such as William Kaufman, Robert Osgood, Henry Kissinger, and Bernard Brodie; and the recommendations for a balanced defence posture appearing in the reports of the Gaither Committee and Panel II of the Special Studies Project of the Rockefeller Brother's Fund.[9]

The quotation admirably sums up the complicated, interlocking nature of the discussions about US national policy that took place in the years preceding President Kennedy's election. It is hard to see how such a major change in national strategy could have taken place without the fullest possible participation by those outside as well as inside the government. It is also apparent that each of the three Services played a crucial role in the public debate. The Army by pressing for flexible response, the Air Force by initiating and, after much discussion, accepting the RAND study on survivable strategic forces, and the Navy by pressing for Polaris, all produced elements in the final policy. Although the arguments may have been to some extent dictated by narrow considerations of Service interest, their contribution to what most analysts of military policy would consider to be a better strategy is incontestable.

Although there have been no major changes in the style of public debate since then, one significant and perhaps alarming development was noted by the magazine *Common Cause* about the campaign by Rockwell Incorporated to reinstate the B1 bomber after it had been deleted from the defence programme by President Carter.[10] *Common Cause* reported that Rockwell contributed $60,000 to political action committees in the 1979–80 electoral cycle for presidential and congressional candidates. Both Republican and Democratic candidates' campaigns benefited from these contributions which were concentrated on those whose districts stood to gain if the B1 programme were restarted. The reelection campaigns of congressional members serving on defence-related committees also received contributions from Rockwell according to the magazine, which goes on to point out that a very high proportion of those receiving these campaign contributions voted for the reintroduction of the B1 bomber. Whatever its merits or defects as part of the political process, the success of this campaign cannot be ignored by any Service that sees favoured weapons projects threatened with cancellation by the executive. Indeed, this campaign can be seen as one example of the so-called iron triangle of Congress, bureaucracy, and special interests to which many commentators refer.

These examples can end on a more positive and encouraging note. After his retirement, General Jones wrote an article for the *New York Times* amplifying his proposals to reorganise the Joint Chiefs of Staff.[11] His article appeared (as these pages were being written) in the *New York Times Magazine* (which British readers could equate to the colour supplements of the quality Sunday newspapers). The appearance of the later columns of General Jones' article beside advertisements with glamorous women in expensive fur coats brings home, to this writer at any rate, the extent of the audience in the United States for such important but esoteric matters as defence reorganisation.

The foregoing analysis in which different parts of the public debate are considered separately is likely to miss the point or at any rate give the wrong impression. Seyom Brown's summary quoted above clearly shows the many strands making up a national policy. But one must also recognise the extent to which the actors themselves change roles. The critic may well become the decisionmaker. The fluid and open nature of the debate, with the barrier between official and nonofficial thought being far from impervious, the constant movement of the intelligent and articulate students and analysts of defence and foreign policy from the outside into government and out again, the whole body of Congress with its powerful committees and shrewd and inquisitive staffs, the private research organisations and the semiprivate "think tanks" staffed by those who have been in government and no doubt expect to be again, all these ingredients of the debate give the discussions a force and a depth not matched in the United Kingdom. Those attacking existing government policy may have been doing so from within government a short time before; those propounding a new policy may have left the administration to do so. If either group succeeds, then they may return to government to carry out their policy. The debates are about real issues, and real power is the prize. It is no wonder that in such a fluid situation the Services see no clear advantage and great potential danger in accepting any loss of their traditional independence.

OPEN OR CLOSED POLITICS?

It is now over twenty years since Lord Snow spoke about the "cardinal choices" for "advanced industrial societies being made in secret by a handful of men who at least in legal form cannot have a firsthand knowledge of what these choices depend upon or what their results may be."[12] In the Godkin lectures where he first put forward this proposition, he went on to illustrate it by recounting the history of the controversies between Lord Cherwell and Sir Henry Tizard before and during World War II about the introduction of radar and the effectiveness of strategic bombing. The historical survey and the general propositions that Lord Snow develops in these lectures are not relevant to this discussion, but it is important to consider first, how far the description above could reasonably be applied to the United Kingdom in the 1980s, and second, to what extent the controversy that his description aroused in the United States was justified and whether indeed it is valid there.

Lord Snow's description of the "closed politics" of the scientific choice of weapons systems[13] has many similarities with the system of Defence by Discussion described earlier in this study as a characteristic feature of defence policymaking in the United Kingdom today. Although, his description does not deal with quite the same issues as those mentioned in chapter 3, where the evolution of Defence by Discussion was briefly narrated, the essence of the bureaucratic politics of each is the absence of appeal to a larger assembly (either of an elite opinion or of the electorate itself). This is not to imply any disregard for democratic ideals by those involved, but simply to argue that the whole style of defence management in the United Kingdom tends to promote decisions secretly arrived at and often secretly implemented. Defence by Discussion therefore tends to imply decisions taken behind closed doors. These doors may be closed because the outsider finds it hard to reach and open them rather than because they are locked from the inside to secure secrecy, but they are closed nevertheless.

It is easy to see why Lord Snow's remarks aroused so much controversy in the United States where they were first made.[14] Not only did they not fit the facts as perceived in post-World War II America, but they seemed to deny the value of the great debates on defence and foreign policy as Michael Armacost points out in disputing the description given by Lord Snow:

> One of the striking things about the Thor-Jupiter controversy was the very openness of many of the discussions and decisions leading to the development and procurement of IRBMs. The evidence of this case suggests that the process of competitive development of weapons by the Services generates determined pressures for the broadening of participation in policymaking, for the illumination of many of the financial and strategic costs and consequences of alternative proposals, and for the transmission of considerable secret information via leaks and counter-leaks to congressmen and the public, thus permitting the intra-executive branch discussion of the issues to be monitored by a somewhat wider alternative and reasonably well-informed audience.[15]

This is an admirable description of the way in which inter-Service controversy over procurement decisions can in the United States widen out so that inevitably, and in US eyes rightly, the discussion of these decisions becomes public. It is true that Professor Armacost is apparently confining his analysis to the United States; but taking Lord Snow to task, he does not apparently consider the possibility that Lord Snow's description of the British scene may indeed be correct. One must conclude that both writers are broadly correct when they describe the way in which decisions about (to quote President Truman's phrase again) "strategy, programs, and budget" are made in their own countries. It is the transfer of the conclusions from one country to another and the attempt to see them as universal that brings error.

CONCLUSION

The closed politics of the United Kingdom, where all attempts to change a government decision on defence must be focused on the cabinet, do not as a rule encourage the Services to widen the debate about resource allocation to include those outside the public service. In the United States it is very hard for the Services to keep the debate behind closed doors, even if they wished to do so. If the Services have strong feelings about a major decision on resource allocation, these sentiments will almost certainly be brought out in congressional investigations and become a matter for public debate.

Chapter Eight
The Bureaucrats

So far this study has been concerned first with the structure of the two defence bureaucracies and then with the extent to which the differences between them can be explained either by the differing internal structure of the government and the legislature or by the differing external environment of public opinion and public discussion in the two countries. It is now time to consider the bureaucrats themselves. As Morton Halperin writes, "there is an unwritten code of ethics which determines at least in part a bureaucrat's behavior." It will be important to see how far the different career structures and attitudes of the two bureaucracies help to explain the differing management styles in the two defence organisations.

A distinction must be made between the formal structure of the organisation for making decisions or solving problems on the one hand, and on the other hand the mental attitudes and bureaucratic skills of those within the machine itself. The former dictates where a problem will enter the machine and how it will be processed; the latter may well influence how it will be solved and what techniques and what kind of analysis will be used as part of the decisionmaking process. Even if the evolution toward Defence by Discussion in the United Kingdom and the continuation of Defence by Bargaining in the United States is largely conditioned by the different structures within which defence decisions are made, it is still important to consider how far the differences between the bureaucrats themselves reinforce this tendency and how far their differing styles of management depend on these differences in the people concerned.

The term bureaucrat, in the sense used here, includes those in uniform as well as those in civilian clothes. No detailed analysis, however, of the military bureaucrats in either country is attempted. Clearly, the military officers of the three Armed Services in the two countries differ from each other in many important respects. But it is the similarities of background, of Service education, and of the career pattern of the military bureaucrat that are most striking when these are contrasted with those of their civilian colleagues.

In both countries the junior officer starts his career in executive positions in military units. Those who reach senior positions in the Defence Departments are likely to have had experience of command of military units at about the rank of lieutenant colonel or equivalent and to have received some type of staff training to fit them for posts in major Service headquarters or in the Defence Department itself. In neither country is the military officer likely to spend all his service, after staff training, in the Defence Department, and in neither will he have had, before his first appointment to that department, to face the problems of inter-Service resource allocation or even be thoroughly familiar with the roles, missions, and problems of the other two Services.

In both countries, therefore, the military officer is likely to arrive to take up his first Defence Department appointment (and probably subsequent appointments also) imbued with a natural and proper ambition to ensure that, as far as lies within his power, his own Service will receive its proper share (one might even say the largest possible share) of the total funds allocated to defence. If, therefore, the Chiefs of Staff Committee in one country play a full and important role in the inter-Service resource allocation process, whereas in the other their opposite numbers play little or no part collectively in the final budget decision, then the reason does not lie in the background, Service education, or career pattern of the military bureaucrat.

One interesting sidelight should be noted, however. General Jones mentioned in his criticism of the defence establishment that officers assigned to duty outside their own Service (and he specifically included service on the joint staff in this duty) do not normally do as well in their subsequent careers as those who have only served in their own Services.[1] No doubt the same thought has occurred to British officers serving on the central policy staffs of the Ministry of Defence; but it is not easy to find examples of British Service officers who have been notably "defence minded" suffering from lack of promotion on that account. In any case, the 1982 reforms gave the Chief of the Defence Staff much greater influence in the selection of senior officers for promotion. The foregoing may seem to imply that the Services in each country share a common pattern of attitudes and methods of work. Such is definitely not the case. Each differs markedly from the other, but these differences are not significant in the context of decisions about resource allocation. The two civilian bureaucracies, however, differ significantly in several ways.

UNITED KINGDOM

The British civil service has been recognised as one of the great political creations of nineteenth century Britain, and in the middle of this century, senior British civil servants were described by a US public servant, who had had extensive dealings with them, as exemplifying "an exceptionally high order of intelligence, extraordinary intergovernmental communication, and general team work and urbanity."[2] There are many less complimentary views of the British civil service whose general merits are not for discussion here, but these remarks do serve to underline two important points. In the first place, the politically impartial, full-career senior civil servant, serving the government in power whatever its political complexion and with wide experience possibly in more than one governmental department, is in a real sense a part of the political fabric, part almost of the constitution, of the United Kingdom. This is not to undervalue the part played by the five or so senior and junior ministers with political appointments in charge of the Ministry of Defence. On the contrary, the small number of ministers appointed by the political party in power emphasises the extent to which the permanent civil service in this and in all government departments consider it their duty to advise on and execute the policies of whichever party is forming the government of the day. In the second place, the cohesiveness of the civil service and the general effectiveness and urbanity of the relations between different government departments are highly relevant to relations between departments within the Ministry of Defence.

The 120 or so senior civil servants[3] in the Ministry of Defence can best be described as long-service officers whose career and training are designed to make them the servants of the ministry as a whole rather than of one particular Service department. This attitude and career policy stem from the fact that all civil servants in the Administration Group are ultimately subordinate to the Permanent Under-Secretary (PUS) and their scientific colleagues to the Chief Scientific Adviser (CSA). The numbers at headquarters in these grades are not large, so that a feeling of loyalty to the department as a whole can be stimulated at this level at any rate.

Before examining the part that these civilian bureaucrats play in the resource allocation process within defence, it will be helpful to consider the central resource allocation process as carried out between the Treasury and other departments in Whitehall to see if this process throws any light on the phenomenon of Defence by Discussion. The larger picture has been interestingly described by two American authors in a book aptly entitled *The Private Government of Public Money*.[4] The "eternal dialogue between the Treasury and the spending departments" over the allocation of resources is discussed in a chapter called, revealingly, "Village Life in Civil Service Society." The authors, Hugh Heclo and Aaron Wildavsky, stress, among other things, the continuity of the dialogue not only throughout the financial year, but through successive financial years (and they might have added, successive financial crises) and the importance that departments attach to building up a reputation with the Treasury for trustworthiness and efficiency. From this it follows that the temptation to "bounce" the Treasury (for example, by withholding unfavourable news while securing Treasury commitment to initial expenditure) or other sharp practice is usually resisted. They suggest that the following rules of the game for getting along with the Treasury would be accepted by most of those involved:

> Consult early and thoroughly;
>
> Rather than trying to hide it, give the costs of a proposal in sufficient depth of years to show if there really is going to be a large charge;
>
> Clear your line before, with other interested departments;
>
> Send extensive information to the Treasury;
>
> In trying to get more, preserve your credibility by dealing in reasonable negotiating margins.

"What is at stake," the authors suggest, "is not merely courtesy and bureaucratic decorum. Experienced members in the tightly knit community value such rules of the game, for they are rules which help them contain very real conflicts and a game about deadly serious questions of public policy."

So much then, in brief, for the rules of the game in dealing with the Treasury. How is this relevant to resource allocation within the Ministry of Defence? Most obviously, if these rules apply to Defence-Treasury dealings it would be surprising if the dialogue about resource allocation within the Ministry of Defence were not conducted by the same or similar rules as those suggested for Whitehall as a whole. This likelihood must be reinforced by the already noted fact that all those senior civilians on both sides of the dialogue in the central staffs and in the service departments owe allegiance to the Permanent Under-Secretary or Chief Scientific Adviser. In short, an unwritten code of ethics as suggested by Morton Halperin in the quotation at the beginning of chapter 5 is discernible in resource allocation discussion in Whitehall as a whole and also in the Ministry of Defence.

Of course, other participants in the discussion—the ministers in charge of the ministry and the Service officers at all levels—will have a profound influence on what is decided. But as has been explained, the individual Service officer, and equally the political minister, do not as a rule serve continuously in the department for more than three years at a time. They are not likely, therefore, to influence the method by which matters are decided as much as those who will sometimes serve for as long as ten years in more senior positions and when replaced will be succeeded by those of similar background and experience and of like mind. The tone of Defence by Discussion is therefore largely set by those civil servants responsible for conducting the financial or budgeting side of the dialogue for year after year, either within the Ministry of Defence (as part of Defence by Discussion) or as a Ministry of Defence representative in discussion with the Treasury (as part of "The Village Life in Civil Service Society").

UNITED STATES

"It was a glittering time. They literally swept into office, ready, moving, generating their style, and their confidence; they were going to get America moving again. There was a sense that these were brilliant men, men of force, not cruel, not harsh, but men who acted rather than waited.... Everyone was going to Washington and the word went out quickly around the Eastern seacoast, at the universities, and in the political clubs, that the best men were going to Washington. Things were going to be done and it was going to be great fun; the challenge awaited and these men did not doubt their capacity to answer that challenge."[5] So David Halberstam describes the start of the Kennedy era and sets a scene that has virtually no parallel in the United Kingdom.[6]

The extensive recruitment of highly qualified staff, frequently with strongly held political convictions, by a new US administration leads to the existence of the "in-and-outer," the man or woman for whom public life and public service will alternate with a career in business, in a profession (the law being of course a particularly obvious example), and last but certainly not least, in academic life. As has already been mentioned, the style and depth of debate of public issues clearly owes much to the people in this category; their contribution to the bureaucratic process will be examined later, but before doing so the staffing position in the Department of Defense must be described in more detail.

Perhaps the best method of comparing the bureaucracies of the two departments is to think in terms of leavening. In the United Kingdom, the bureaucracy is leavened by five or six political appointments on each change of government. The holders of these positions will speak for the department in cabinet and its ministerial committees and in Parliament. The remaining senior civilian staff, some 120 in all, will consist almost wholly of long-service civil servants whose career is likely to be within the Ministry of Defence or in other government departments, but not outside the civil service.

In the United States, the 1,400 or so senior posts[7] are leavened by some 120 noncareer appointments. About thirty of these are appointed by the President and consist of the most senior posts from the Secretary of Defense down to (in United Kingdom civil service terms) deputy under-secretary. They are likely to leave when the President leaves office. A further ninety noncareer executive assignments are usually made to key appointments at a lower level (say, under-secretary and assistant secretary in UK civil service terms). Their duties will involve both the framing and the advocacy of policy. Not all these will change with each administration, but most will probably do so. The remaining 1,280 senior civil servants will be part of the Senior Executive Service likely to complete their careers in government service.

Already, the contrast between the US and UK bureaucracies is plain. The in-and-outer holds a key position in the Department of Defense, filling (if one includes the top political appointees; such as Secretary of Defense, Deputy Secretary of Defense, and the Service Secretaries) all senior policymaking posts in the department down to assistant secretary (in US terms) level. A significant number of in-and-outers will be in the Directorate of Defense Research and Engineering and in the Directorate of Program Analysis and Evaluation: two of the key directorates in the Office of the Secretary of Defense concerned with resource allocation. The third directorate in the Secretary's office involved in this task is the Comptroller's office, which has primary responsibility for the defence budget; this office has only a few noncareer civil servants (but this number may well include the top two posts). The large number of career officers in the Comptroller's office somewhat redresses the balance between career and noncareer personnel in the field of resource allocation, but the contrast with the UK Ministry of Defence is still a sharp one.

An incoming Secretary of State for Defence has only some four, or at most five, political colleagues to assist him in implementing his party's policies. His opposite number at the start of a presidential administration will have about 120 posts at his disposal. Those coming to very senior defence appointments will not, as a rule, be slow to use the power to make new subordinate appointments in the Defense Department after their arrival. Whatever their own views about the advantages of continuity and experience, they will face strong pressure from those expecting appointments either for themselves or their nominees.

But this is not a static situation, and recent events in the United States have tended to blur the sharp contrast between the two bureaucracies. First, Hugh Heclo, whose perspective on the British civil service was mentioned earlier, has pointed out that the in-and-outer is changing. He has identified a kind of professional in-and-outer who has become more prominent as the role of the political parties and their patronage has declined.[8] The essential characteristic of these "public careerists" is previous and generally relevant experience in government. Professor Heclo has calculated that about half of President Reagan's top appointees in the winter of 1980–81 had held subordinate appointments in previous administrations. This is not to suggest that they are following a well-marked-out political career like the British member of the House of Commons (or House of Lords) who hopes to climb the ladder from Parliamentary Under-Secretary, to Minister of State, and then to Secretary of State. On the contrary, the only career planner for the public careerist can be himself.

There are clearly enough of these public careerists to justify classing them as a de facto higher civil service. As Heclo emphasises, "what the public careerists will know about the ins-and-outs of government work and their own networks of personal contacts in Washington help this de facto higher civil service use, if not administratively control in any classic bureaucratic sense, the machinery of government." The proviso, however, is all important from a defence point of view. Despite his previous experience, the public careerist will probably not remain for more than two years on average in one position, and this period is not long enough to learn to manipulate the intricate machinery of financial management and budgeting described in the next chapter.

The second development is easier to describe but harder to evaluate. The Civil Service Reform Act of 1978 (CSRA) made some major changes in the federal civil service. The Act established a Senior Executive Service (SES) for top administrators, instituted merit pay for middle-grade managers, and created a statutory basis for labour relations in the federal sector of employment. As Mark Huddleston has pointed out, however, "by vesting most of the functions of the old bipartisan Civil Service Commission in the newly created Office of Personnel Management (OPM), the CSRA redefined the lines of authority, placing most responsibilities firmly in the hands of presidential representative's."[9] This change could have serious implications for the Senior Executive Service, which now must be considered in more detail.

The Senior Executive Service was intended to be an elite cadre of the 8,000 or so mostly career, supergrade bureaucrats in federal employment in levels GS-16 through GS-18, the top three rungs of the US civil service with some 150 in the bottom two levels of the Executive Schedule. The British equivalent to the Senior Executive Service would be those in the Administrative and Scientific Civil Service down to and including assistant secretary. The plan was for those holding the top political appointments in each government department (very broadly, political appointments in the British system) to choose their own senior staff teams from among SES employees, who would be encouraged to move to new jobs and to gain greater expertise by special financial bonuses and the prospect of a wider range of appointments in government departments.

The Senior Executive Service has not, by most accounts, been a complete success. Some 95 percent of those eligible joined the Senior Executive Service, but the Office of Personnel Management (the successor to the Civil Service Commission) admitted in 1981 that morale was low and many were leaving the service mainly because of congressional limits on the size of salaries and the number and size of bonuses that SES employees could earn. Even if pay and bonus levels could be restored to keep pace with inflation, there would still be another difficulty to overcome. At least part of the impetus for the 1978 Act was the desire to make the permanent civil servant more responsive to political direction by allowing incoming presidential appointees to select subordinate staff from a wider range of civil servants instead of virtually having to accept the incumbent in post. This point and the dangers that could result from it are convincingly developed in Professor Huddleston's article, already mentioned. An article that appeared in the *National Journal* at the time puts civil servants' fears very vividly:

> But on the other side, detractors of the President's plan fear that the Senior Executive Service reform will accomplish exactly what the civil service system is supposed to prevent—the intrusion of partisan politics and personal favoritism in the selection of top employees and the administration of federal programs. Instead of a highly professional, highly motivated cadre of federal managers, they foresee a group of timid toadies who will blow with the prevailing political wind because they know that their political bosses have the power to dispatch them to lesser jobs on what many call the "turkey farm."... They believe that the new system will make it much easier for an unscrupulous administration to politicize the bureaucracy.[10]

William Lanquette reported in 1981 that "SES members feared that although no one has been demoted from the service, the 1978 reform has left their political overlords with the power to abuse their rights."[11]

There is no evidence that such fears have been realised, and there are indications that career civil servants are now less fearful of relegation to the "turkey farm." As regards the Department of Defense, the number of policymaking posts held by senior career civil servants is about the same as in 1976, and the loss of senior staff before retirement has not been significant.[12] If, as will be suggested in chapter 13, the two essentials for those senior civilian bureaucrats dealing with resource allocation problems are continuity and calibre, then the position regarding the former has not been improved over recent years, and the latter may well be eroded if the low SES morale means that good-quality candidates are not recruited to the civil service. Nevertheless, the 1978 Act provided the legislative basis for improvements from which the Department of Defense budgeting system could benefit greatly if the circumstances were right.

A COMPARISON OF MANAGEMENT STYLES

The next two chapters will discuss to what extent recent major innovations in defence management are the natural and obvious products of the bureaucracies that invented them; but some illustration of the different management styles used by the two bureaucracies may help to make the same point. Many writers have stressed the extent to which UK government business, including defence business, is conducted by committees, which can be seen as the natural method of working for a permanent bureaucracy. Most key issues of defence business are likely to be decided either in a formal committee or in an informal meeting of those closely concerned; and if they are not decided there, then previous meetings will almost certainly have had a decisive influence on the final decision.[13] In the US Department of Defense, it seems to be a far less common practice to reach decisions in a committee meeting. As one senior official put it, "we have committees alright—plenty of them, but we tend to use them to get the people concerned to reveal their position on an issue. The key decision is probably reached by telephone calls between the three or four most important people after the meetings."

Another interesting feature for the outside observer is the important part played by special appointments to what would be known in the United Kingdom as the private office of senior staff both in the Department of Defense and elsewhere in the federal government. Many of the most senior staff appear to retain their own circle of trusted aides and advisers to protect themselves as it were from the bureaucrats. No doubt this is a natural reaction to those coming as in-and-outers to senior positions, but the results of these appointments can be significant as a former public servant has pointed out:

> The deputy, the special assistant or aide, disposed a subtle power in government. No policy was purely theirs alone, yet the bureaucrats below could not propose without going through them, and superiors rarely decided without them. In the trust and sheer proximity of the decision-maker, theirs was the power to shade, to change, to initiate, and, even more formidably, to delay, to plant doubts or nuance or complexity blanched out by a bureaucracy abhorring and ignoring them all, to protect the boss from blunder by stampede or default of independent judgment. Most of all, the power was *part* of the process, symbiotic in the organism of policy, inseparable—mainly because if the aide were not so intimate and crucial, he would be replaced by someone to fill that necessary role [italic in original].[14]

This description of the Pentagon of the sixties appears to be still valid twenty years later. It has no parallel in the British system, where the minister's private office will be almost wholly staffed by permanent civil servants, whose powers are far less significant.

Finally, the lack of permanent cadre in the most senior ranks perhaps goes some way to explain the lack of attention to long-term planning and the apparent lack of interest of the US bureaucrats themselves in any major reorganisation proposals that might overcome the adversary relationships between the Services. One former civil servant has remarked that in his experience most internally inspired reorganisations in the Defense Department were designed either to increase the responsibility of an individual office holder or to diminish it by isolating him from information and access. It is a notable fact that, apart from the initiative by General Jones in 1982, the impetus for most defence reorganisations in the United States came from outside the US defence bureaucracy, whereas the UK defence bureaucracy can claim credit for many of the changes effected in the last forty years.

CONCLUSION

The main characteristics of the two defence bureaucracies are now clear. In the United Kingdom, the defence bureaucracy is a close-knit (and possibly to outsiders, homogeneous) body of permanent civil servants with some five or six political appointments at the head of it. In contrast, the outside observer receives a clear impression that the defence bureaucracy in the United States is dominated by the in-and-outer. This impression may derive not only from the thirty senior posts appointed by the President but also from the ninety noncareer executive assignments at a lower level, most of whom will be replaced by each new administration. The creation of the Senior Executive Service has not changed the dominant position of the in-and-outer, including the public careerist. Not surprisingly, the two bureaucrats with different backgrounds go about their work in different ways.

Chapter Nine
Financial Controls and Budgetary Procedures

The career patterns and work methods of defence bureaucrats in either country are clearly different and contribute to the differing styles of defence management. These correspond to Morton Halperin's unwritten "rules of the game." It is now necessary to study those procedures and techniques that are adopted more formally for the despatch of business. Because the bureaucrats differ both in background and career, it seems likely that the controls and procedures that come easily to one nation's bureaucrats will not be so readily adopted by the other.

Before considering the two sets of budgetary procedures—Planning, Programming, and Budgeting System (USA) and Public Expenditure Survey (UK), which dictate to a considerable extent the way decisions on resource allocation are handled, it would be well to analyse in more detail the controls that the two legislatures exercise over defence spending. In both democracies, civilian control of defence is complete, and, not surprisingly, from the earliest times the democratically elected assemblies have exercised their authority over the executive by resorting to the power of the purse, but they have used it in different ways.

UK PARLIAMENTARY CONTROL OF EXPENDITURE

Since 1706, a House of Commons standing order has laid down that only the Crown (or in modern terms the executive) can make proposals to Parliament of expenditure. Erskine May[1] puts it even more decisively: "A charge cannot be taken into consideration [by Parliament] unless it is demanded by the Crown or recommended by the Crown." Thus, because, generally speaking, the party in power is the party controlling a majority in the House of Commons, the government's control over expenditure proposals should be absolute. Their proposals for expenditure on defence should be presented before the financial year in question, and they should be able to ensure that the House of Commons (the House of Lords does not have a say in proposals for expenditure) will vote the necessary money when it is required.

Parliament is provided with a Defence White Paper setting out the government's policy for the coming year and with Defence Estimates setting out in broad terms under subject or vote headings the exact sums required. The Estimates may provide useful information but are in no sense a means of detailed control. Nearly one-third of the defence budget will be contained in vote 1, whose all-embracing title was in 1981, "Pay etc., of the Armed Forces and Civilians, stores, supplies, and miscellaneous services." The total is admittedly broken down into some twelve subheads, but the government may during the year switch money from one subhead to another without the prior approval of the House of Commons; therefore, this additional information is not suitable for detailed control. Similarly, the second subject heading in vote 2 is simply entitled "Defence Procurement": it does not give in its ten subject headings any detailed costings for individual weapons systems or any indication of what financial commitments are entailed in future years by weapons programmes proposed in the current Estimates.

The House of Commons will, of course, have each autumn the government's Public Expenditure White Paper providing projections of, amongst other items, total defence expenditure for the next three years. But the House of Commons is not asked to approve the detail of this White Paper in any formal fashion, nor does it have any place in Parliament's mechanism of audit and control of expenditure. This White Paper is informative not normative.

US CONGRESSIONAL CONTROL OF APPROPRIATIONS

In the United States, the executive and the legislature share responsibility not only for the allocation of funds to defence but also for the way funds are shared out among the Services and their weapons programmes. Originally, Congress itself drew up the budget and decided how to raise the necessary revenues, but since 1921 the President has been responsible for preparing the defence and other Estimates. Nonetheless, the power to decide is still shared and Congress must agree not only to the total but also to each item, paying particular attention, not surprisingly, to those items that will commit the executive to further expenditure in following years. Indeed, the whole apparatus of congressional control bears upon the point where the executive creates an obligation through contractual action involving personal services or material. The control of outlay (that is, cash flow) is a secondary consideration. Congress gives New Obligational Authority (NOA) with single-year or multiyear appropriations, broadly as follows:

Military Construction	5 year appropriations
Shipbuilding	5 year appropriations
Other Procurement	3 year appropriations
Research and Development	2 year appropriations
Operations	1 year appropriations

Under this system, the obligation or contract for the item must be entered into during the appropriation life, but the money need not be wholly spent during that period. Since the coming into force of the Congressional Budget and Impoundment Control Act of 1974, the President has been required to submit five-year departmental budget projections with his annual request for funds, but these projections are used for information only; they are not authorised by Congress as such. The linked system whereby the House and Senate Armed Services Committees grant authority for an activity, before Defense Appropriations Subcommittees of the House and the Senate grant funds, ensures that the emphasis remains on future obligation for, rather than on annual, expenditure.

Congressional control of outlay is, by contrast, weak; there are no formal sanctions against overspending in any one year of defence expenditure. The congressional resolution on outlays aggregates all federal expenditure, and administrations have in recent years overspent or underspent the defence budget by as much as $2 billion for reasons not directly connected with defence.[2]

One other feature of the American scene should be noted. Congress is not compelled by its own rules to authorise appropriations for defence (or any other) expenditure before the start of the fiscal (in the UK, financial) year on 1 October. If an appropriation bill is not passed by Congress on time, then the executive can only incur new financial obligations up to the level specified by a continuing resolution of Congress. In recent years the federal government has had to become accustomed to living with continuing resolutions. Thus, in 1982 Congress did not approve the President's request for defence funds for fiscal year 1983 before 1 October, and authorised funds for defence technically ran out on 17 December. Finally, Congress passed a further continuing resolution for $232 billion on 21 December despite President Reagan's request for $250 billion. Among the items deleted by Congress from the President's request were production funds for the MX and Pershing 2 missile programmes.

Defence officials in the United States have been heard to speak with wonder and envy of the ease with which their British colleagues can get budgets approved by the legislature. At the same time, they are mystified by a system of control that appears to place little or no legislative limit on the extent to which the administration in power can commit future defence expenditure. They see, in short, a system in which the British legislature does not demand by law but gets by courtesy, as it were, a fairly reliable forecast of total defence expenditure for the next few years (namely, the Public Expenditure Survey) and, in contrast to their own Congress, concentrates on annual outlays one year at a time. Congress devotes much attention to obligation for future expenditure, but is unable to form a clear picture of total defence spending in future years because the executive and the legislature can only agree on expenditures one year at a time. It now remains to examine the two contrasting internal systems of budgeting, Planning, Programming, and Budgeting System (PPBS (US)) and Public Expenditure Survey (PES (UK)), to see how these affect the process of resource allocation.

PPBS AND OUTPUT BUDGETING

The introduction of the PPB system (PPBS) as a budgetary procedure by Mr. McNamara was described in chapter 4. Alain Enthoven has written: "The fundamental idea behind PPBS was decisionmaking based on explicit criteria of the national interest in defence programs, as opposed to decisionmaking by compromise among various institutional, parochial, or other vested interests in the Defense Department."[3] He goes on to emphasise that this system entailed first considering military needs and costs together and then explicitly choosing at the top level between alternatives. Clearly, therefore, the PPB system was seen, quite rightly, as being more than an information system or a method of organising data for analysts to work on; nevertheless, the essence of the system is the display of data describing program packages that represent in theory a common defence mission. This part of the system will now be considered, and to distinguish it from the PPB system as a whole, the term "output budgeting" will be used on occasions to describe both the US and UK version (which is normally referred to as the functional costings). In the original program analysis of the US defence budget, some ten programs covered such items as Strategic Retaliatory Forces and General Purpose Forces. These programs have changed somewhat since they were introduced for fiscal year 1963, but the basic approach and the main programs still remain (see table 9.1). From the start, therefore, the data has been laid out without regard to the Service providing them; and this gives the clue to the main purpose behind the system.

Before his inauguration, President Kennedy appointed a committee headed by Senator Symington to study the organisation of the Department of Defense. The Symington report, published in late 1960,[4] criticised defence planning as representing at best "a series of compromised positions among the military services," which was because the Joint Chiefs of Staff had to act both as defence planners and as representatives of their Services. The committee recommended far-reaching changes in defence organisation designed to insulate defence planners from the parochial thinking of the Service departments. The incoming Secretary of Defense did not, however, accept the proposed reorganisation.

Table 9.1
PPBS Programs and Functional Analysis

	USA PPBS	UK Functional Analysis	A Possible Revision (see chapter 13)
1.	Strategic Forces	Nuclear Strategic	Nuclear Strategic
2.	General Purpose Forces	Navy General Purpose Combat Forces	European Theater Ground and Air
3.	Intelligence and Communications	European Theater Ground Forces	Rapid Deployment Force Including Sea Lift, Air Lift, and Reserve Stocks
4.	Air Lift and Sea Lift	Other Army Combat Forces	Maritime Forces
5.	Guard and Reserve Forces	Air Force General Purpose Forces	Home Defence
6.	Research and Development	Reserve and Auxiliary Forces	Intelligence and Communications
7.	Central Supply and Maintenance	Research and Development	Central Supply and Maintenance
8.	Training, Medical, and Other General Personnel Activities	Training	Central HQ and Administration
9.	Administration and Associated Activities	Repair	Research and Development
10.	Support of Other Nations (excluding MAP)	War and Contingency Repairs	Miscellaneous
11.		Other Support	
12.		Miscellaneous	

He saw himself as an active rather than a passive manager, a leader not a judge. Early in his term he said: "I am here to originate and stimulate new ideas and programs, not just to referee arguments and harmonize interests. Using deliberate analysis to force alternative programs to the surface and then making explicit choices among them is fundamental."[5] The introduction of the PPB system in general, and output budgeting in particular, must be considered with this statement in mind.

The fundamental purpose of the PPB system at the start was not to create new ideas about defence policy or strategy, because the incoming administration had already made up its mind about many of the major issues of defence policy before assuming office; in any case, a system for displaying data could not have produced new concepts of military strategy out of a void. But, and this is the important point, the PPB system enabled the administration to have its proposals examined and discussed by the bureaucracy in a context and in an environment that gave these ideas the best chance of success. Any improvements to or acceleration of the Polaris programme, for instance, would under the PPB system be considered not in the context of the Navy's desire for additions to the carrier fleet, but against Air Force requirements for Minutemen.

To some extent, therefore, the system of output budgeting enabled Mr. McNamara to avoid the defects in organisation mentioned by the Symington committee, without making the changes they proposed. As Allen Schick writes:

> PPB and departmental reorganization can be regarded as partial substitutes for one another. When PPB was flourishing in the Defense Department it was utilized to accomplish many of the objectives that had been sought in earlier reorganization attempts. Even though each of the military services retained its separate organizational identity it was possible for the Secretary of Defense to make cross-cutting decisions by means of the mission-oriented program budget. The Air Force had charge over Minutemen and Navy over Polaris, but both were lodged in the strategic forces program. In this way it was possible to overcome internal organizational constraints within DOD without having to engage in what probably would have been a futile battle to abolish the tri-Service structure.[6]

But even if output budgeting was a useful tool at the start of the McNamara era, is there reason to think it will still be useful when it has been transported either through space (for example, to UK defence or to US nondefence institutions), or through time (to US or UK defence today)? Many would answer with a confident "no" and point to the apparent failure of the PPB system to be effective elsewhere in the US federal government.[7] The Department of Defense, however, still retains the system and evidently has no plans to discard it, leading one to believe that in defence eyes the PPB system is still relevant even if it does not command the same prestige as in the past. The answer to these conflicting points of views lies surely in the foregoing examination of Mr. McNamara's use of the system.

The success of the PPB system in the wider meaning of that phrase (which combines planning and output budgeting with cost effectiveness analysis), when coupled with the McNamara style of active management, lay mainly in the field of strategic weapons. Output budgeting was a useful method of getting the Department of Defense to assess the cost effectiveness of one strategic nuclear weapon system against another, instead of letting each Service try to decide whether to forego strategic nuclear weapons in favour of, say, more weapons for conventional war. Whenever output budgeting can present budget or other financial information in a helpful way that would not otherwise be readily obtainable owing to the particular shape of the organisation in question, then it can be of great use to the active manager. If, however, the organisation is perfectly fitted for its budgetary task, or if the budget is merely divided out among the component parts of the organisation for them to spend as they wish (as will probably be the case in Defence by Bargaining), then this method of presenting information has a less important role to play.

It can therefore be argued that the PPB system can still play a role in US Defense where the organisational defects cited by the Symington Committee (and later by the Blue Ribbon Defense Panel and other committees of inquiry) are still evident. Its failure elsewhere in the US federal government can be ascribed to a number of causes,[8] but the two preconditions for success—namely active management in the McNamara style and an organisation not precisely fitted for its budgetary task—are not perhaps always present. The relative lack of success of the UK equivalent, namely, the functional costings, is also explicable in these terms. It is not as necessary as it was in the United States in Mr. McNamara's time, because the relevant information for crucial decisions can be extracted from an organisation geared more to Defence by Discussion than Defence by Bargaining. Functional costings, therefore, were, and are, used more for purposes of presentation in connection with the annual Defence White Paper; but should the need arise, variants of them could no doubt be used as an essential tool for long-range planning and decisionmaking in the United Kingdom.

So far as it goes, the foregoing explanation of the use of output budgeting in both countries seems broadly correct, but it clearly does not do justice either to the enthusiasm of the talented men who first introduced it into the Pentagon or to the high hopes some still have for its future development. Part of the explanation for the high hopes at the beginning has already been mentioned. The PPB system was not just a method of displaying data but the essential prerequisite for a meaningful analysis of military needs, because force requirements and budgetary limitations could for the first time be combined into one system. So PPBS, as the phrase implies, is a Planning, Programming, and Budgeting System which, its inventors would no doubt argue, made the budgetary process work much more effectively than in the past. But there is another, more fundamental, reason for high hopes then and for some confusion now.

Any system of output budgeting is only as good as the categories or outputs or costing functions chosen. If these categories are relevant to the analysis to be done and the decisions to be made, then the PPB system will be generally hailed as a success; if they are not relevant, then its value is likely to be questionable. In the McNamara era, the program categories separated the strategic nuclear elements of the budget from the expenditures required for conventional war. Much important analysis in this field could therefore be accomplished and vital decisions made and accepted by all concerned. But it also seems to have been assumed over the years that one unique set of program categories or costing functions could serve all future analytic needs. In fact, as Allen Schick points out, "there are as many ways to classify information as there are analytic perspectives."[9]

Although well-fitted to help in analysing strategic nuclear problems, the original PPBS program categories of the 1960s and 1970s could not be used so effectively for dealing with conventional war. Thus, to take an obvious example, one category covered general purpose forces, including those to be used in the land/air battle and those destined for maritime operations, and some of the logistic support for these forces was separated from the forces for which they were intended. It would therefore be very difficult to study, for example, the cost effectiveness of tactical air in support of ground forces on the basis of these categories as they stood. A different analytic perspective, concentrating on conventional war problems, would require that the information be set out in a different way. Perhaps some of the failure to analyse many of the problems of conventional war effectively, stemmed from the natural reluctance of the bureaucracy to make radical changes in the program elements once they had been adopted, after a considerable struggle to get them accepted and understood in the first place.

Another barrier in the way of change was the desire to use output budgeting not only as a basis for long-range planning and budgeting, but also as a tool for day-to-day management of current operations, using that word in its widest sense to include not only military operations of war but also the management of every aspect of the armed forces in peace. There was a natural desire to use the PPBS programs for the control of expenditure on current operations so as to get some check on the accuracy of the budget forecasts and proposals for future expenditure. Unfortunately, the dilemma posed by this objective seems insuperable. If output budgeting is to be used for the analysis of future needs and the evaluation of future options, it must be flexible enough to change when the planners perceive that those needs have changed or when new options come to their notice. If, however, output budgeting is to be used also as a tool for audit and a check on past expenditure, then the output functions or programs chosen must remain unchanged for several years, at least while they are assimilated at every level both inside and outside the central defence organisation, so that costs wherever incurred can be ascribed with certainty to their correct program and function by every clerk in the financial machine. There seems to be no way of providing one set of programs that are flexible enough for planning purposes and at the same time stable enough to be used for day-to-day management and audit.[10]

The British experience with output budgeting would seem to support this view of the advantages and disadvantages of the system. The United Kingdom adopted output budgeting as part of the format of the Defence White Paper shortly after the introduction of the PPB system in the United States, but the system has not become a basis of defence planning as it was in the Pentagon in the McNamara era.[11] It could hardly be so. The twelve functional programme headings used resemble those in the US program budget although the problems faced by UK defence planners are rather different (see table 9.1). Thus, strategic forces form one major function, and the conventional forces for the Navy and Air Force form two more. The Army combat forces form two separate functions, one devoted to European theatre forces and one to forces for other theatres. Yet, the critical choices faced by the United Kingdom in the field of defence for most of the intervening period have not been about which and how many competing strategic nuclear weapons systems (for which the PPBS categories in either country are well adapted); instead, the choices have been between which and how many conventional weapons systems can be accommodated within a limited defence budget; for these choices a different set of costing functions would be needed.

Granted, then, the gradual decline in the utility and prestige of output budgeting in defence on both sides of the Atlantic, and ignoring the far broader question of its utility in other fields of government expenditure, can it be sufficiently improved to be useful in dealing with current and future defence problems? Clearly, it would be essential to realise that no one unique set of costing functions will be relevant for all times; if the needs of the planner are to be met, these functions may have to be changed as often as the problems facing him change. From this it follows that an output budget which suits the planner will not be permanent enough to be useful for financial control and subsequent audit of current operations. The needs of day-to-day management must be met by a separate categorisation of the defence budget; this categorisation could be based on inputs (such as manpower, equipment, and supplies) or outputs (such as strategic forces and general purpose forces), whichever is most suitable. Such headings should not be subject to frequent change if they are to be assimilated, as they must, at all levels in the machinery of financial control and audit.

If, then, change is desirable, what changes should be made? Surely they should be designed to take advantage of the success already achieved with the aid of output budgeting; namely, the analysis of strategic options in the field of nuclear weapons. The aim should be to seek other self-contained areas that could become separate program categories in a revised layout. Two such areas immediately spring to mind; the first is maritime operations in a general war in which ships and aircraft will be engaged together in a conflict against similar forces and weapons on the opposite side. The second is land/air operations against an enemy employing sophisticated weapons in both elements. For all practical purposes, and certainly insofar as the acquisition of modern and complex weapons systems by both the United Kingdom and the United States is concerned, this means maritime operations on the high seas and land/air operations in Europe against the Soviet Union. The extent to which analysis of the cost effectiveness of weapons in these two program categories will help decisionmakers will be considered in chapter 13, but at this stage the argument is that new costings functions should be devised if full and proper use is to be made of both output budgeting and the PPB system in the widest sense of that term. The two suggested, together with the existing strategic function, will be found to contain most of the expensive and complex weapons systems which absorb so much of the defence budget and about which agonizing choices have to be made.

PES AND LONG-TERM BUDGETING

Whereas the PPB system was an American invention applied with only partial success in UK defence planning, the Public Expenditure Survey (PES) is a wholly UK contribution to budgetary planning at the highest level; the Public Expenditure Survey has no exact counterpart in the US federal government. The following paragraphs are mainly concerned with the extent to which the budgetary and planning procedures adopted throughout Whitehall affect planning and resource allocation in the Ministry of Defence. They also consider briefly the extent to which the United States has adopted comparable methods. It is in many ways misleading to think of long-range planning in general, and the Public Expenditure Survey in particular, as something the UK Ministry of Defence was slow to adopt. As has already been noted in chapter 3, the ministry adopted a system of forecasting future expenditure, known as the long-term costings, in the mid–1950s, and by the end of the decade, ten-year long-term costing was an established feature of defence budgeting; but although it was used by both the Ministry of Defence and the Treasury, it was not at that time widely adopted elsewhere in Whitehall.

However, in 1961, as a result of the Report of the Committee on the Control of Public Expenditure chaired by Lord Plowden,[12] annual long-term costings were started under Treasury control by all major spending departments in Whitehall. These costings are now known among civil servants as PESC after the committee of officials responsible for coordinating the Public Expenditure Survey of future government expenditure, which has been published since the late 1960s. It is not necessary to enter into the details of this procedure for setting out the future cost implications of all current government policies, but two points should be noted. First, the simple phrase "the future cost of current policies" clearly contains ample room for disagreement between spending departments and the Treasury; what may seem to the spending department to be a logical consequence of a past policy decision, may to the Treasury (particularly if it involves a vast increase in expenditure) appear to be a radical change of policy requiring special approval, perhaps by ministers. Second, it should be emphasised that it is not the task of the survey committee to allocate resources among the spending departments; this allocation is, as always, a matter to be settled bilaterally between the department and the Treasury and if necessary referred to the cabinet for a final decision. The survey committee is concerned with coordinating the result of such discussions and matching this result to the national resources likely to be available, as well as with establishing a rational basis for financial forecasts throughout all government departments.

The effect of this PES revolution on the Ministry of Defence itself is of some importance. It might be thought that the introduction of the Public Expenditure Survey represented a setback to the ministry since it lost much of the autonomy in the field of long-term budgeting that it previously enjoyed. However, there is a great advantage in the present system for which many former defence planners and members of finance branches would have been ready in the past to sacrifice much—that is certainty, or rather a greater measure of certainty in an uncertain world. However precise and well argued the long-term projections may have been in pre-PES days, they did not finally commit the Treasury and rival spending departments to any particular level of defence spending in the future. Now, by implication, the general level of defence spending for a period of, say, three years is accepted by all concerned in government, because other government departments by accepting their own share must logically accept the correctness of the share allocated to others. More important, by publishing the Public Expenditure Survey, the government of the day commits itself, as far as any government can or is prepared to, to a planned level of defence spending for about three years ahead. None of this provides absolutely certainty; financial crises and changes of government are bound to entail major reviews of defence spending. Indeed, to those closely involved in forecasting for the Public Expenditure Survey, the picture will no doubt appear to be constantly changing, as indeed it is, since changes are frequently made at the margin, often to provide funds for nondefence expenditure that is urgent or has a high political priority. Nevertheless, to a large extent the future is structured. Major items of expenditure can be phased so that all do not peak at the same time, and once the budgets for new weapons systems are fixed, they tend to remain immune to cancellation or major reductions during subsequent reviews. Moreover, the public debate over the share of gross national product to be allocated to defence has had one result in the past; the percentage share tended to remain at a particular level for some years, thus providing the planner with some measure of certainty.

Indeed, the extent to which the PES machinery has tended to grind on without regard to national economic circumstances and the need to control inflation is emphasised by the criticisms that W. A. Godley and others made to the Select Committee on Expenditure in 1975–76, showing the extent to which under the Public Expenditure Survey the Treasury found it almost impossible to exercise close control of departmental expenditure.[13] In the past, departments had been virtually able to ignore the effects of inflation by calculating the cost of their policies and programmes at constant prices for the survey. Any increase of costs due to inflation had then to be added to the annual Estimates when presented to Parliament. One unhappy result of ignoring inflation in order to obtain stability in the planning of policy had been to weaken government control of total spending, thus encouraging a rate of inflation that was too large to be ignored in the planning process.

In 1976–77, the government took the first steps to rectify the situation by imposing cash limits on all current public expenditure that was not demand determined (such as social security payments, which are set by statute). A limit was thus placed on the total sum that could be spent in any one year on defence (with certain minor exceptions, such as service pensions). If prices rise faster during the year than is allowed for in the cash limit for defence spending, then the Ministry of Defence must reduce expenditure by the necessary amount to compensate for the difference, even if it means cutting previously approved programmes. The discipline of having to manage within a fixed sum was not a new experience for long-serving MOD officials who could remember the 1950s and before, when the annual peacetime Estimates as agreed by Parliament has indeed seemed fixed and immutable. It was an unwelcome shock for some of their younger colleagues, accustomed to presenting supplementary Estimates to Parliament during the course of the financial year and supporting these proposals with the perfectly reasonable argument that prices had (or would) rise faster than was allowed for when Parliament approved the original Estimate.

Annual cash limits may have been unwelcome to defence planners, particularly after 1979–80 when the annual Estimate was presented to Parliament at cash-limit prices, but it did not seriously hinder the planning process. The next step taken to increase control of public expenditure was more serious. In 1981, the government decided that all forward planning under the PES system should be expressed in cash rather than in volume terms at constant prices. This decision meant that when the Public Expenditure Survey was being prepared, all departments had to cost their policies and programmes at current prices and then increase their bids for future years by whatever allowance for price inflation over the PES period was set by the Treasury. Central finance departments in all countries tend to underestimate future rates of inflation, therefore, defence planners naturally fear that the defence programme will be subject to a hidden cut each year because the Treasury will not make adequate allowance for future inflation, and defence spending will have to be cut to make up the difference between the estimated and the actual rise in prices. Because these cuts would have to be carried forward into future years, the cumulative effects could in theory negate sensible long-term planning. That has not happened so far, but cash planning, as it is called, must be regarded as a retreat from pure PES doctrine even if it is justified in the wider context of government financial policy. Some commentators have seen cash planning as a fatal blow to the PES system. This is discussed more fully in chapter 13. Here it is sufficient to point out that those who operate the present system believe in its value and to that extent at least it can be said to work.

A useful consequence of the introduction of the PES procedure has been that in UK defence planning the arguments about resource allocation often concentrate on years three to five of the long-term costing rather than on expenditure for the year about to begin. Long-term costing has two advantages. In the first place, when economies have to be made, it is often possible to plan these economies for a period three to five years ahead by concentrating on long-term projects, such as closing depots or running down manpower, instead of having to take last-minute cuts in the coming year's budget, which can normally only be achieved either by slowing down current production of weapons or by reducing the amount to be spent on building projects. Long-term planning therefore makes it easier to make rational economies, but it also, and this is the second advantage, often makes these economies more tolerable. If adequate notice is possible, manpower reductions can be achieved by wastage instead of by dismissal; and if weapons systems are to be cut from the inventory, it is often easier to persuade the unlucky Service to give up a weapon system planned for the future rather than one that is in service or just about to come off the production lines. Long-term planning can mean more rational cost-cutting and may also make the economies achieved more acceptable to all concerned.

There are, of course, superficial similarities in the budgetary procedures in Britain and the United States, but the less obvious differences are particularly interesting. First, the analysis of the place of the defence budget in relation to the rest of UK government spending is paralleled by the examination made for the President by the National Security Council (NSC) of the total US defence budget in relation to the remainder of federal spending.[14] But this process differs significantly from the Public Expenditure Survey. The NSC report to the President is not binding on anyone and cannot decide, let alone impose, any balance between defence and nondefence spending. The President has this prerogative, and he cannot effectively delegate it to any subordinate group. Furthermore, the National Security Council cannot make a decision about the level of the budget over a period of years; the decision about the level of federal expenditure is shared between the President and Congress, and they have not in the past shown a willingness to commit themselves jointly for more than one year at a time to any particular level of spending either for defence or for all government activities.

Nevertheless, the Defense Department has for some time now produced for Congress five-year projections of that part of defence expenditure which will be committed by congressional approval of the budget for the coming fiscal year. Congress is therefore able to see the implications of defence projects that are just starting and can thus fulfill its responsibility for approving the executive's requests for projects whose costs will in part be incurred in succeeding fiscal years. These requests for New Obligational Authority are, as has been mentioned, taken most seriously by Congress, and congressional committees examine witnesses from the Defense Department to see to what extent these requests for funds in the coming fiscal year commit the future. But, except in this area, neither the executive nor the legislature has as yet shown a desire to be jointly committed to any particular level of defence spending in the future; therefore, neither the Department of Defense nor the individual Services have any firm and congressionally agreed allocation of resources for future years. The DOD five-year defence plan of future defence budgets is never published. Unlike the United Kingdom, therefore, inter-Service arguments in the United States about the allocation of resources tend to be about provision for the coming fiscal year, and not about allocation in the longer term where it might be possible to make more rational decisions, which also might be more acceptable to the loser.

The 1974 Congressional Budget and Impoundment Control Act was designed to overcome a number of the problems resulting from this sharing of control over the federal budget between the executive and the legislature. The new procedure came fully into force for the 1977 fiscal year, and the Congressional Budget Office, created by the act to serve the House and Senate Budget Committees, has produced valuable studies of budgetary problems. It is also clear that Congress does look at both the outlays and revenues of the federal budget together instead of piecemeal as in the past. This approach is an advantage for the defence budget because it restricts those congressional committees that have in the past voted to increase certain areas of defence expenditure without either making compensating savings elsewhere or imposing additional taxes. However, the defence budget, in common with other parts of the federal budget, can still face serious problems with the legislature, particularly when the President and the congressional majorities are from different political parties. The final session of the 97th Congress in December 1982 (described at the start of this chapter) provided a notable instance of this difficulty, which led to despairing press comments about the ability of Congress to deal with budget problems.[15]

Since 1978, there have been some moves toward long-term financial planning. In 1981, Congress agreed to the administration's proposals that multiyear procurement be introduced for certain weapons systems, thereby enabling larger numbers to be ordered at one time, thus reducing the unit price of each. This is a small but useful step toward securing some degree of certainty about the future defence budget. In 1977, Dr. Rivlin, the Director of the Congressional Budget Office, recommended multiyear budgeting, arguing that this would give Congress more time to scrutinize expenditure.[16] Since 1982, both the Senate and House Budget Committees have approved defence budgets for two years beyond the financial year in question, but these budgets have not formed a satisfactory basis for long-term planning because apart from anything else they have not been accepted by the administration. The inherent difficulties in this process were stressed in 1983 by the Bipartisan Appeal on the budget crisis (a prestigious group led by five former Secretaries of the Treasury), which pressed for reduction in federal expenditure in defence and in other areas to reduce the budget deficit. They pointed out that Congress was in favour of defence cuts and warned of the danger of "relentless ad hoc tinkering with dollars and programs that will fatally sap the coherence and capabilities of our military forces for years to come." They went on to "urge the President and congressional leadership to join together in supporting a bipartisan resolution that commits the nation to a more gradual but significant and sustained increase in the defense budget for the next several years." This resolution would not, the group admitted, be legally binding but would, besides having other benefits, "permit more coherent planning of the defense effort."[17] If the United States does not yet have any sound basis for long-term financial planning for defense, many persons with great experience in this field clearly see the great dangers in the present annual budget battle over defence without any agreed long-term plan.

CONCLUSION

The projections of future defence expenditure produced in each country differ significantly. They were devised in different environments and are used for different purposes. In both countries, those concerned with defence policy use forward projections to ensure that current plans for future expenditure are both consistent one with another and practicable. However, in the United Kingdom, the Public Expenditure Survey gives a public commitment by the government about the future level of defence expenditure. This commitment does not have the force of law and does not commit future governments, particularly those of a different political persuasion; but it has the prestige of the government of the day behind it and has proved in the past to be a reasonable basis for long-term planning.

In the US government five-year defence plan, which is not even published, there is no such commitment for the future, and the 1974 budget reforms have not yet altered this. The US system has clear advantages for financial control by the legislature, but the ad hoc nature of the system should not be overlooked. Recent UK experience has shown that the Public Expenditure Survey was not an ideal tool for financial planning at a time of high inflation; nevertheless, defence planners must accept that the attempt to improve the system by introducing "cash limits" planning is far preferable to no long-term financial planning at all.

Both departments use similar systems of output budgeting, but this procedure has in the past proved more successful in the United States than in the United Kingdom. The reasons for this are discussed in more detail in the next chapter.

Chapter Ten

Management Techniques

The UK and US defence organisations use many management techniques and aids to decisionmaking. Only two, however, operational research and systems analysis, appear to bear closely and decisively on the types of decisions about resource allocation that are the subject of this study. There are strong arguments for saying that both operational research and systems analysis are part of a continuous spectrum of techniques, starting at the lowest level of complexity with engineering analysis and finishing at the highest level with various forms of policy analysis.[1] Others would no doubt argue that both terms refer to much the same thing and distinctions such as are proposed here between the British and American versions only make a confusing subject yet more confused. Neither country, of course, has a monopoly of any of the techniques covered by these headings. Further, in neither country is a hard and fast distinction made between operational research and systems analysis, which in the US terminology shades off into policy analysis.

Nevertheless, strong arguments exist for discussing the two techniques separately. The act of introducing these techniques into the field of defence policymaking has profound implications for the politics of the decision process. Because the defence organisations of the two countries are different, the place of the analyst in the organisation and the tasks that he is given may well be different. A brief survey of the origins and achievements of each technique should help to explain this difference and perhaps suggest some pointers for the future. Operational research is considered first because, historically, it preceded systems analysis.

OPERATIONAL RESEARCH

Operational research (OR) had its origins in the World War II studies carried out in connection with the installation of radar and the subsequent studies of antisubmarine warfare in the Bay of Biscay and Atlantic from 1941 onwards. These milestones are clearly important in the history of analysis, but it should be remembered that as early as 1916, F.W. Lanchester published *Aircraft in Warfare*[2] in which he not only sought to define the proper role of aerial bombardment in attacks on the enemy homeland, but also suggested the famous Lanchester equations that are still the basis for many computer simulations of armed conflict. It is interesting to note that Lanchester dealt with both the strategic aims of air warfare and the problems of combat between armed bodies of men, which have since become two separate areas of discussion.

The first, the strategic use of bombers, was a matter of intense discussion in the United Kingdom at the highest level during World War II. But as C. P. Snow remarked, "even in 1942 it was just an unrationalised article of faith that strategic bombing was likely to be our most decisive method of making war."[3] The analysis used by Lord Cherwell and his staff to support the arguments for area bombing of German cities, even though successful in that the policy was adopted, is not now claimed as an example of successful operational research. First, the argument ignored the resource cost of the proposal and failed to prove that such a policy was the most effective use of the resources consumed. Second, the effect of general area bombing of German cities was seriously overestimated. Although this estimate was a matter of intense debate at the time, it could not be confirmed until studies of German cities took place after the war.[4]

From 1944 onward, the bomber offensive was directed more toward oil and communications targets and less to the large urban areas—the targets proposed by Lord Cherwell. Lord Zuckerman, then scientific adviser to Air Marshal Tedder, was one of the foremost advocates for the bombing of communications targets, which as subsequent studies showed had been most effective in Italy and France. This change of emphasis brought greater success, but still the impression remains that analysis of strategic bombing of the enemy homeland was not an area in which British operational researchers felt confident of producing their best work; their subsequent accounts of World War II tend to concentrate on other matters.

Thus, in recounting the role of operational research in World War II, Lord Zuckerman suggests three categories of analysis:[5] First, the problems of introducing new weapons—the example he gives is the introduction of radar; second, the tactical consequences of new and complex weapons—the classic example is the analysis of antisubmarine warfare, proving that convoy losses could be minimised if the size of convoys were increased; and third, what actually happened in a military operation as opposed to what was supposed to happen—here he quotes the examination of bombing in Italy, already mentioned, as providing an important corrective to bombing policy. He also mentions the unrealistic estimates of the navigational accuracy and destructive power of the bombers with which Britain entered the war.

This retrospective view of the role of operational analysis by one who was later to be Chief Scientific Adviser in the Ministry of Defence was influential and widely shared, but two points are worthy of comment. The first, its concentration on tactics and weapons rather than on strategy, has already been noted. The second is as important; World War II analysis seems to have ignored resource costs by concentrating, as Lord Zuckerman has recognised, on making the best use of weapons either in or just coming into service. Thus, the North Atlantic convoy study, by concentrating on the combat between escorted convoys and U-boats, failed to discern, or at any rate to analyse, the true purpose of the operations: presumably the most efficient method of transporting supplies across the ocean. In this wider context, which would have been apparent if resource costs had been recognised as a factor, the possibility of rerouting the convoys would have been considered and some limit on the size of convoys would have been suggested if, as seems probable, the limited capacities of ports of arrival and departure would have entailed long delays of very large convoys before transhipment.

One vital point was evidently grasped at an early stage, namely, the need for the analyst to become involved in the decisionmaking process if his studies are to be used. This involvement was achieved in the Royal Air Force (RAF) by trying to ensure that the civilian head of operational research in an RAF command had access to the commander and worked closely with the operational staff.[6] In this way, scientific staffs were fully exposed to all aspects of the operational problems on which they were to offer advice, and because of their right of access to the commander in chief, they could ensure that their advice was not suppressed at a lower level.

The post-war history of scientific advice to the Services in the United Kingdom must be dealt with briefly. This is not to suggest that no advances in skills or organisation have been made since then; indeed, the contrary is the case, and one important innovation is discussed below. However, it is suggested that Service acceptance of the scientist and vice versa in the United Kingdom was, and perhaps is still, based on the successes both achieved together in 1939–45 and tends to ignore areas, such as strategic policy, in which they had been unable (no doubt due in part to the lack of time) to produce results during World War II. There are two more points to note. First, more scientific manpower in the Ministry of Defence is devoted to monitoring the development of new weapons systems than to the study of strategic or tactical doctrine in the abstract, and these studies did not in the early years place much emphasis on cost effectiveness. Second, the implications of introducing scientific advice into defence decisionmaking were not overlooked. Just as in World War II the scientists had tried to ensure that they had direct access to the commander in chief, so in peace the right of the scientific advisers in the three Service departments to have direct access to the committees corporately responsible for those departments (now known as the Service Boards) was confirmed.

The post-war development of defence operational research paralleled the development of the defence organisation as a whole. The analysts working in this field were a part (and a relatively small part) of the defence scientific staffs and worked until the 1964 reorganisation exclusively for one of the three Services; the only exception was the staff attached to the Scientific Adviser to the Minister of Defence, but this staff did not carry out OR studies, such as wargaming, on its own account. Before considering the consequences of the 1964 reorganisation, it is important to note one development that was not necessarily implicit in the wartime experience that has been outlined. The Army Operational Research Group was established at West Byfleet near London after World War II, and one of its early tasks was to study weapons and tactics by means of simulations of the land battle.

This revival of interest in wargaming, which has a history going back to antiquity, was paralleled in the United States and seems to have been due partly to the advent of nuclear weapons and partly to the development of new conventional weapons, such as the antitank guided missile, which made assessment models based on the tactics and weapons of World War II unrealistic. It is unnecessary for this study to trace the growth of this type of simulation on both sides of the Atlantic and the part that computers now play in it. However, the way in which those responsible for this type of simulation were organised in relation to the Ministry of Defence is certainly important and provides an interesting comparison with US practice.

The key date in this context is April 1965. As part of a plan to combine the OR efforts of the three Services, the Defence Operational Analysis Establishment (DOAE) was established at West Byfleet. The change of title from "operational research" to "operational analysis," besides being more explicit, avoided confusion with another branch of the ministry dealing with operational requirements; despite this potential source of confusion, the original title will be retained in this study, as it has been both in industry and in defence outside the United Kingdom. A more important change was indicated by the substitution of "Defence" for "Army." Officers from the other two Services joined what had previously been a small, but important, Army nucleus in a mainly civilian staff, thus increasing its potential to become a centre for analysis for all three Services. The benefits of inter-Service cooperation in this field may have been slow in appearing, but by 1974 a model of the land/air battle in Central Europe had been sufficiently developed for some assessment to be made of the influence of tactical air forces on the land battle. This assessment could provide important guidance on alternative force structures and procurement options for ground and air forces. The establishment has also devised a maritime model to assess sea and air forces and to analyze alternative force structures and weapon mixes. The analytic staff of this establishment can therefore now consider and advise on a scenario involving two (or more) of the Services.[7] The DOAE staff, both service and civilian, work together on the tasks given to the establishment.

This defence, as opposed to single-Service, analytic capability could be of importance because of the strengthening of the defence, as opposed to single-Service, scientific capability at the Ministry of Defence since the 1964 reorganisation. As noted in chapter 3, the Chief Scientific Adviser can call on all scientific staff at all headquarters and research establishments for information and advice, in the same way as the Permanent Secretary can control and coordinate the work of nonscientific civil servants in the ministry. Through the chairmanship of such important committees as the Defence Equipment Policy Committee and the Defence Research and Intramural Resources Committee, and representation on the Operational Requirements Committee, the Chief Scientific Adviser and his staff are in close touch with the latest developments in weapons development and procurement. They should therefore be able to initiate studies and reviews to provide new insights into resource allocation problems.

A considerable analytic capability is thus available to defence policy-makers. The relative freedom of this capability from the direct influence or control by any of the three Services may well have been important in the past and could be even more so in the future. In 1981–82, the House of Commons Defence Committee made special mention of DOAE in its second report and urged that its role and scope be enhanced, possibly by centralising all operational analysis resources, building on DOAE's established capability and "proven record of rigourous and impartial analysis."[8]

SYSTEMS ANALYSIS

This method of approaching problems is derived from operational research as practised in the United Kingdom during World War II. By 1945, both US Armed Services had OR advice available to them. The Army Air Force was probably the greatest user of operational research and, interesting to note, in 1944 started a major study of strategic bombing in preparation for a final, conventional bomber offensive against Japan. The interest developed by this study may well have led the Air Force in 1946 to establish project RAND, out of which grew the present Rand Corporation. As Donald Rice has written, "RAND was conceived in the mid-1940s as a way to continue the partnership between the nation's military leaders and its scientists who had contributed so much to ending the last war."[9] Project RAND was originally intended to be a programme of scientific study and research on the broad subject of air warfare with the object of recommending to the Air Force preferred methods, techniques, and instruments for this purpose.[10]

The defence headquarters organisations in Washington were also eager to receive scientific advice throughout the post-war period. A Research and Development Board was established in 1947. This function was assigned to the Assistant Secretary (Research and Development) in 1955, and in 1958 to the Director of Defense Research and Engineering. In the same year, as a result of the Sputnik crisis, the Advanced Research Projects Agency was created to avoid duplication in the development of strategic missiles. In addition, numerous ad hoc scientific committees were set up, the most famous of which were the Von Neuman (1954), Killian (1955), and Gaither (1957) committees. Moreover, President Eisenhower's creation of the post of Scientific Adviser to the President helped to ensure that scientific advice on defence matters did not get ignored at lower levels.

However, the arrangements thus far described for providing scientific advice to decisionmakers do not help explain why systems analysis as a particular set of techniques, or more properly as a way of approaching problems, emerged in the United States rather than in the United Kingdom. The arrangements at headquarters were broadly similar in both countries, although, not surprisingly, on a more lavish scale in the United States; and in both countries scientific advice concentrated initially on the same sorts of problems. It is true that the extramural capability the US Air Force had established at RAND had no direct parallel in the United Kingdom, but it did not for the first few years apparently produce any work radically different from that undertaken by scientists in World War II. The engineering approach at RAND concentrated at that time on weapon design and effectiveness without considering cost. It was, however, from RAND that the decisive change of direction in defence analysis was to come.

In 1947, a conference of social scientists met in New York to discuss how their disciplines could best be used by RAND; subsequently, economists (among them Charles Hitch, later Comptroller of the Department of Defense) were recruited to the corporation. An early study, completed in 1948, of possible new long-range bombers for the US Air Force, is generally recognized as the first occasion on which cost-benefit analysis was applied to the description of a strategic bombing system. A subsequent and more famous study, RAND 266, the Strategic Bases Study, which originated in 1951, was largely the work of Albert Wohlstetter, a consultant, and Henry Rowen, an economist.[11] One can conclude, therefore, that there was an appreciation of resource limitations and a willingness to apply sophisticated economic techniques to US defence problems some ten years before Mr. McNamara introduced these techniques into the Pentagon.

The significant difference between UK operational research and US systems analysis was therefore established with recruitment of economists to RAND. This is not to imply of course that in the United Kingdom the scientific staff in general, and those engaged in operational research in particular, were not conscious of the cost of weapons and of the limit on the size of the defence budget; but in the early days, for a number of reasons, their advice and analysis were not always brought to bear, on either side of the Atlantic, at the point where decisions were made on resource allocation. It is now necessary to see how this was effected in the United States and how, to put it another way, systems analysis the technique became the Office of Systems Analysis (OSA) the organisation.

The previous chapter has already stressed the extent to which the Planning, Programming, Budgeting System (PPBS) was used as a substitute for a reorganisation of the Pentagon. Mr. McNamara wished to ensure that the options on force structures and the decisions on the purchase of major weapons came to him so that he could consider like with like (for example, US Air Force strategic nuclear weapons with US Navy Submarine Launched Ballistic Missiles, SLBMs), instead of considering weapons choices and force-levels, Service by Service. Clearly, the technique of systems analysis was a vital part of this process of comparing competing options within the same program. Indeed, cost effectiveness analysis can be said to be the main justification for the PPB system; there is little point in compiling data in the form of program elements if the data compiled with such effort is not going to be subject to scrutiny and analysis in that form.

Granted the validity of the techniques, it is first important to ask why Mr. McNamara, having foregone the opportunity to reorganize the Department of Defense (DOD) and instead chosen PPBS/systems analysis to achieve control, decided to change defence organisation by introducing a separate group of people to carry out these analyses. It would have been more in keeping with his objective to have required the existing bureaucracy to adopt systems analysis rather than to have introduced outside experts as a separate group. In a sense, the answer is contained in the conclusions already reached about the PPB system. As Robert Art writes:

> The revolutionary manner in which McNamara made his decision. . .transformed the "expert" career bureaucrat into the "novice" and the "inexperienced" political appointee into the "professional." By demanding that decisions be made through a cost effectiveness analysis, McNamara freed himself from the Secretary's usual depend-

> ence on the experience and knowledge of the military officer and the career civil servant. By demanding something that only he and his small personal professional staff possessed the experience and competence to do, McNamara declared insufficient or invalid, or both, the customary criteria for making decisions and the traditional grounds for justifying them.[12]

Therefore, no emphasis was placed, either at the start or later, on training the career staff of the Comptroller's office for this type of work. The necessary specialists were brought in to carry it out. At the start in 1961, there were six staff, with no direct responsibility for decisions on resource allocation, who undertook long-range studies in depth. But the Office of Systems Analysis grew dramatically over the years until it numbered some fifty people in 1964 and two hundred by 1968. By then, it held wide-ranging responsibilities that were probably not even guessed at by the original six analysts.

It is useful to trace the steps by which this handful of experts became the Office of Systems Analysis, the organisation in the Department of Defense with considerable powers of financial control over defence spending. The contrast with the scientific staff of the UK Ministry of Defence, who have no financial or other direct management responsibilities for the total defence budget, is most remarkable. At the start, the OSA staff had a close relationship with Mr. McNamara, could approach him directly, and responded quickly to his requests. Clark Murdock quotes one of them as saying: "It was a bright group of people who could put together analysis in a hurry, did data digging, was action oriented.... So the limits of Systems Analysis' responsibilities were determined by the personal tastes of the Secretary of Defense."[13] By responding to the needs of the Secretary of Defense, by collecting data and getting their work to him before the long-established and slower moving parts of the department, the Office of Systems Analysis became, or tried to become, an extension of Mr. McNamara himself. In consequence, they quickly achieved a position without a parallel in the more homogeneous bureaucracy of the British Ministry of Defence. The nearest comparison, and by no means a good one, is with the Central Policy Review Staff in the Cabinet Office in the United Kingdom, which was abolished in 1983.

After the PPB system was installed in 1962, it became necessary for the Services to submit Program Change Proposals (PCPs) for any significant change in authorised policy. If these proposals involved force structures, they went to Systems Analysis for scrutiny, and Mr. McNamara would tend to accept their advice. At a later stage, they became responsible for writing most of the Draft Presidential Memoranda, described in chapter 4, and in 1964 the Office of Systems Analysis started to produce annual Tentative Force Guidance tables, which became in effect the authorised force guidelines on which all planning should be based. The JCS Joint Strategic Objectives Plan (JSOP) was thus superseded, and the Office of Systems Analysis (with a staff of about fifty) had changed from being a reviewer of Service proposals to being the basic force planner for the whole system, in that it controlled the important numbers in the US force structure.

The final step in the transformation from systems analysis to Systems Analysis came in 1965, when Charles Hitch was succeeded as Comptroller by Robert Anthony. At that stage, the post of head of the Office of Systems Analysis was upgraded to Assistant Secretary of Defense (Systems Analysis) with a rank equal to that of the Comptroller and with, of course, complete independence and free access to the Secretary of Defense. Systems Analysis was fully, and apparently irrevocably, a part of the bureaucratic machine. A major change had been made in DOD organisation, a change that the Services much resented, and it would be idle to pretend that as a result of the change the bureaucratic machine worked smoothly during Mr. McNamara's time.

The root cause of the trouble was surely the break between planning and budgeting. Congress has always insisted on the submission of annual budgets and was unwilling to accept budgets submitted in the program categories devised for the PPB system. The budget staff in the office of the Comptroller therefore continued, as in pre-McNamara days, to get budget submissions from the Service departments. These submissions were organised on an input basis according to appropriations categories (such as operations, procurement, and personnel), and the Comptroller's department was responsible for preparing the submission to Congress (as part of the President's budget) in the traditional form. There were thus, in effect, two sets of financial controllers: the systems analysts and the budgeteers; but as one analyst quoted by Clark Murdock said: "The real crunch is the budget and the real king is Comptroller. You can write all the DPMs and five-year plans, but what really counts is who gets the money. In the budget crunch, SA fights like hell with the Comptroller. After fighting the Services in the programming stage, they have to fight in behalf of the Services for funds for the approved program. The Comptroller still makes the hard decisions."[14]

The speaker was dealing with the period 1964–67, but in one form or another the lack of coordination, or even conflict of interest, between the Comptroller's department concerned with the budget and those in Systems Analysis concerned with the analysis of longer term force structures and weapons projects has persisted, although Mr. Laird's emphasis on participatory management (discussed in chapter 4) helped to ease this particular problem. After Mr. Laird's time, the prestige and power of Systems Analysis has fluctuated, but on the whole Clark Murdock's analysis remains the correct one.

It is important to note three areas in which this break between planning and budgeting had unfortunate effects. At a fairly early stage, the Office of Systems Analysis became responsible for dealing with Program Change Proposals and Draft Presidential Memoranda; the former authorised changes from established policy suggested by the Service departments, while the latter laid down new policy on major issues and were initiated on the authority of the Secretary of Defense himself. Both have budgetary implications, and when it came to cuts in the budget, the Comptroller did not feel himself committed to either. As time went on, therefore, the Program Change Proposals were not submitted until the budgetary review was in full swing (in the autumn of each year), and over half the decisions on them were not made until after decisions on the budget had been made. In other words, the decision by the Comptroller's office was crucial, not the OSA decision. In the same way, the Draft Presidential Memoranda prepared by the Office of Systems Analysis could not be used by the Service departments as a firm basis for budget submissions because they were drafted before the final decision on the total defence budget had been made.

A second casualty in this situation was the five-year defence program. This program has already been discussed in the context of the UK Public Expenditure Survey, but it is important to note the consequences for the Office of Systems Analysis. The unwillingness of Congress to commit funds for more than one year (except in the narrower context of New Obligational Authority), and the extreme difficulty of the executive in making firm plans for future expenditure, mean that the Comptroller's long-term plan is the five-year defence program, which is approved by the Secretary of Defense but not published or approved by Congress. In consequence, the Comptroller cannot recognize any long-term planning commitment as a firm commitment to any level of future spending. Therefore, to cite an analyst interviewed by Clark Murdock: "No one is very straight about what the meaning of a five-year program really is. RAND said we needed it for costing weapons systems; but a five-year program is not really a number of approved programs but a guess about budget levels."[15] The validity of long-term planning on this basis is clearly suspect and some, at least, of the difficulties of the Office of Systems Analysis during the McNamara period can be attributed to a growing recognition of this fact.

Finally, this catalogue of problems caused by the split between planning and budgeting should mention the myth of the unlimited budget. The theory of a comprehensive PPB system must surely imply that what is planned and programmed as an element in an approved functional costing will find a place in an approved budget and thus be funded. At the start of the McNamara era, there was indeed an implicit assumption that no arbitrary limit would be placed from outside on the defence budget, but, on the contrary, the Secretary of Defense would see to it that the total of the President's budget would be increased to cover all programs that the Secretary had previously approved. Theoretically, therefore, the sky was the limit for defence spending. Not surprisingly, this state of affairs did not really exist. Research by John Crecine[16] and Clark Murdock shows that, in fact, policy decisions entailing additional funds were not normally given until Mr. McNamara had a general idea, within $1 or $2 billion, of the size of the total defence budget for the coming year; indeed many decisions were not made until the final budget total was known in late December.

However, it would be unwise to attach too much emphasis to this particular facet of the McNamara system of management. Indeed, to the extent that his system served to open up debate between the Services, it clearly served a useful purpose. During the 1950s, the Services had developed a strong hold over the allocation of resources for defence; and to a great extent, the allocation to each was the result of bargaining between the participants, but the way in which each Service spent its share of the budget was largely left to that Service. Mr. McNamara's philosophy of active management clearly required that he intervene not only in the allocation among the Services but also in the way each Service spent its share. It was therefore necessary to induce the participants to discard the positions they had achieved by implicit bargains with their competitors and to persuade them that as far as their own share of the defence budget was concerned the sky was indeed the limit. In these circumstances, each Service would be likely to enter into a debate with no holds barred, with the result that each Service might propose more effective ways of undertaking roles and missions that had previously been the preserve of another Service.

The inception of the Polaris force cannot be credited to this particular debate. However, it is probable that the willingness of the US Navy to commit additional funds to successive SLBMs owed much to their expectation that this commitment would not prejudice other naval programs because additional funds would be provided for in the defence budget to cover this project. To some extent, therefore, the myth of the unlimited budget was useful. Indeed, other Defence Secretaries in both countries have since adopted a variant of this tactic; they have held back a proportion of the available budget at the planning stage so that when the final budget is being assembled, this portion can be allocated to projects that are valuable from a defence as opposed to a single-Service point of view.

Laurence Martin has noted that the greatest apparent successes of PPBS and systems analysis came in the field of strategic nuclear deterrence.[17] It is worth considering why this should be so. Clearly, studies of the cost effectiveness of strategic weapons and related analyses relying on quantitative techniques were convincing and served to raise the level of debate or at least free it from some of the bitter inter-Service rivalry characterising the Thor/Jupiter controversy.[18] Mr. McNamara's insistence that those concerned should think quantitatively played a big part in this success, which in turn relied for success on a generally agreed idea or "model" of the conflict in which the weapons would be used. If no such common perception had existed amongst those who debated both deterrence theory and the acquisition of strategic weapons, and if they had not recognised that strategic nuclear weapons were in a very real sense "different," then it is hard to see how they could have achieved the analytical breakthrough.

This is not to argue that any one numerical model, computer-based or otherwise, can represent to the satisfaction of all (if that can be considered the "mot juste" in connection with so awful an event) the detailed actions and counteractions involved in a possible nuclear exchange between two superpowers. Nevertheless, the basic idea implicit in the phrase "nuclear exchange" is shared and commonly accepted among those who think about the subject. For this reason, debate (which is at times almost theological) about various aspects of deterrence can proceed from a firm and common base. For instance, the broad implications of the options of flexible targeting presented by Mr. Schlesinger in 1974[19] can be readily understood by all concerned and the debate can proceed. To a large extent, therefore, the success of cost-effectiveness analysis in the field of strategic weapons rested on the relative ease with which the outcomes of alternative choices could be gauged from a commonly accepted model.

By contrast, there is no such generally agreed model of conflict in conventional war or in counterinsurgency operations. Success or failure of any particular weapon in a land/air battle between opponents with advanced industrial technologies to support them is a matter of constant debate and argument despite the many conflicts involving conventional weapons since 1945. Similarly, war at sea and operations against guerrillas, or other unconventional forms of conflict, are resistant to modelling or simulation and hence to analysis as convincing as that made for the strategic exchange.

It may be argued that the lack of examples and experience of nuclear war gives a spurious air of certainty to the "model" of the strategic exchange, and if analysts had actual experience to work on, the strategic debate would be as cloudy as the discussion of a conventional war. This argument is hard to accept in this extreme form, but for purposes of the present discussion one need not debate it at all. The almost universal acceptance of the model of the strategic exchange, whether this acceptance was justified or not, gave power to the systems analysis studies of strategic weapons.

CONCLUSION

The present chapter has established that the success or failure of the various techniques discussed cannot be considered in isolation but only in the context of the particular organisations employing them. Management tools of this nature are rarely neutral; their introduction into an organisation will affect the balance of power. Before they are accepted, they will therefore be carefully examined by a bureaucracy that is likely to resist any change affecting the status quo. Operational research was introduced into the UK defence system in time of war and has been accepted since then as one of the tools to help Defence by Discussion. Even if operational research has had no successes comparable to those achieved by systems analysis on strategic nuclear weapons, the Defence Operational Analysis Establishment has developed models of land/air and maritime conflict that could illuminate future discussions about conventional weapons.

By contrast, systems analysis owed its dramatic successes to the fact that it suited the style of the defence manager, Mr. McNamara, who was dominant at the time it was introduced. His style of active management needed a new tool of measurement, which systems analysis provides, to assess conflicting arguments from different Services. Because his successors have generally favoured participatory management and the Service departments have each acquired their own analytical capability, the prestige and authority of the Program Analysis and Evaluation Office (the new title of the Office of Systems Analysis) has in general diminished despite a revival of its fortunes during the Carter administration.

The McNamara combination of PPBS and systems analysis is not suited to Defence by Bargaining. The decline of systems analysis has been accompanied by an increase in the independence of the Services, with the result that conflicting analyses of the same problem could well be produced by two Services when they are competing for the same allocation of funds. Nevertheless, systems analysis in the field of nuclear strategy can be rated as a highly successful product of the environment in which the United States conducts defence business. The next chapter will try to carry this discussion further by considering to what extent inter-Service rivalry is still a significant factor in the decisionmaking process.

Chapter Eleven
Inter-Service Rivalry Over Weapons Innovation

The two preceding chapters have shown that the United Kingdom and the United States go about the business of defence planning and budgeting in very different ways. For one country to borrow wholesale the techniques or organisation of the other, would certainly be frustrating and possibly harmful. The task of translating new management procedures from one organisation to the other is the equivalent not of giving a dose of medicine but of effecting an organ transplant. However, even if it is useless to ask whether one defence organisation is better than the other, some general comment may prove instructive.

One significant difference between the two systems of defence management is the greater independence of the US military services. They are able to argue their case both in private and in public with a freedom denied to their colleagues in Britain and this leads, save in exceptional circumstances, to a system of Defence by Bargaining. The pluralism of the American political process in a real sense requires that the independent voice of each Service be part of the debate, and a number of writers[1] have argued that rivalry between the Services is a great gain because both Congress and the public at large can be kept informed of controversial issues when policy is at a formative stage and can thus exert an influence on the outcome. Increased centralisation of defence planning would, according to this argument, stifle debate and thus lead to the suppression of new ideas. The extent to which inter-Service rivalry enhances civilian control in the US system of government is a matter of opinion, but the belief that it does so is held in influential quarters and fosters the independence of the three Services.

The argument that increased centralisation stifles innovation is of more general interest and must be considered further. Any large organisation of a hierarchical nature is likely to be hostile to new ideas, particularly those affecting established procedures. New techniques are likely to upset the established order, a vital aspect of Service life; and for this reason, if for no other, the military system tends to reject and ostracise the unconventional.[2] However, inter-Service rivalry in the United States has clearly contributed to the vigour of the public debate of defence issues, and in two instances at least has been the means by which defence policy has been changed for what many would consider to be the better. Thus, the US Army by criticising the official doctrine of massive retaliation was in conflict not only with the US Air Force, whose cherished doctrine this was, but also with the US government and therefore the President and commander in chief himself; yet in the end, defence policy was modified to meet the criticism.

Another notable result of inter-Service rivalry was the US Navy's development of the Polaris weapon system. The project was initially pursued by the Navy alone and received little or no encouragement from the Secretary of Defense until the feasibility of the smaller nuclear warhead and the solid propellant was established. The Navy can claim the credit for taking the vital first steps, despite the lack of support from the rest of the Department of Defense (and no doubt that Service would wish in turn to pass much of the credit to Admiral Rickover).

A common factor in both these examples goes a long way toward explaining the Services' vigour in pressing their points of view. At the time in question, both the Army and the Navy were alarmed at the increasingly dominant position of the Air Force in US defence. The largest share of the defence budget, and the only significant role in any future war, seemed logically to belong to the Air Force. The two Services reacted in different ways—the Navy by developing a competitive strategic missile system for themselves, the Army, particularly after the curtailment of the Jupiter programme, by attacking the strategic doctrine on which Air Force dominance was based. Both the Army and the Navy were probably right in their objections, but it is questionable whether either would have pressed the case for their alternative strategy to a successful conclusion unless they had considered that their own interests as a Service would be seriously threatened by failure to do so.

It is very difficult to find convincing examples of the beneficial effects of inter-Service rivalry where major Service interests were not threatened either by a cut in their budget or a reduction in their role. On the contrary, the Blue Ribbon Defense Panel quoted a number of examples where Service parochialism had led to duplication (see chapter 4). In addition, there are instances (such as the failure of the Navy to provide fast deployment logistic ships for the Army) in which projects funded by one Service mainly for the benefit of another fail to receive adequate support from the Service paying for them.[3] At one stage when Mr. McNamara was Secretary of Defense, the US Navy was reluctant to fund the Polaris programme and would have preferred to spend the funds on replacing units of their surface fleet.[4]

Mr. Schlesinger was at one a time an advocate of inter-Service rivalry as an aid to innovation on grounds similar to those just discussed,[5] but later apparently modified his views. In his first report as Secretary of Defense, he stressed that the budget and planning guidance given to the Services each year by the Office of the Secretary of Defense was one of the main ways to "strike the right balance between the beneficial effects of decentralization and inter-Service competition and the adverse effects of inter-Service redundancy and excessive rivalry."[6] Clearly, under this formulation of the argument in favour of inter-Service rivalry, much emphasis is placed on guidance from above, particularly in relation to decisions about allocating defence funds. Put more crudely, this argument amounts to saying "let the Services argue among themselves as much as they like about who does what; they will not be allowed to spend defence funds on doubtful projects unless the budgetary planning guidance permits them to do so."

However, before accepting this judgment on the conflict between centralisation and Service autonomy, further discussion is needed. Above all, one would want to see how it would work in practice. If the guidance from the Office of the Secretary of Defense is to bite, then it will almost certainly have to disallow some cherished projects and probably insist that other projects be included in a Service budget contrary to the wishes of that Service. Certainly, the Defense Guidance issued before a PPBS cycle in 1982 was considered to be too general to prevent the Services from pursuing projects they favoured even if the Secretary of Defense gave them a lower priority.[7] When evidence is available that the Secretary of Defense has achieved results of this order, then two alternative explanations of this event will have to be considered.

Under the first alternative, the position of the Secretary of Defense himself would be so strong that he would have achieved a position comparable to that of Mr. McNamara of whom Robert Art wrote: "He also asserted that any analytic technique can yield only so much information. . . . it is necessary for a decisionmaker to make judgments, and that his perspective as Secretary of Defense made his judgments the most valuable and valid for his job. In order to innovate, McNamara had to take the initiative."[8] Defence by Bargaining would have been superseded, temporarily at any rate. The alternative explanation is even more illuminating. If the planning and budget guidance can achieve the results specified when the Secretary of Defense sees his job as being one of reconciling conflicting Service views, then the United States will have adopted a system of Defence by Discussion almost indistinguishable from the model that should exist under ideal conditions in the United Kingdom. The Services will have renounced their freedom to decide broadly what projects are to be included in their share of the total defence budget.

The idea that the UK and US systems of defence management might be converging is a novel one. Before considering the idea further, it would be well to recall the salient features of the UK organisation for defence planning and budgeting,[9] assuming that this organisation is working as intended. Responsibility for planning falls in the first instance on the central defence policy staff consisting of Service officers with close links to civilian administrators and scientists. These officers prepare papers for the Chiefs of Staff (and subsequently for the Secretary of State) in which they are required to give the best possible overall defence viewpoint, identifying separately, if necessary, individual Service views. This ideal may not always be achieved in practice, but the fact that the Chief of the Defence Staff is responsible for producing a defence view rather than a series of single-Service views, and that his staff are now organised with this task in mind, significantly increases the prospects of success.

The policy staff maintains close links with the Defence Secretariat, nonscientific civil servants who report to the Permanent Under-Secretary of State and who have the primary responsibility to him for long-term financial planning and control, and with the defence scientific staff, who report to the Chief Scientific Adviser. The defence policy staff is therefore at the heart of the planning process. Although planning and budgetary guidance for the long-term costings (and therefore the defence input to the Public Expenditure Survey is the responsibility of the civilian Defence Secretariat, they are bound to keep in close contact with the Chief of the Defence Staff; they could not therefore, in the nature of things, issue guidance widely at variance with the policies agreed by and for the ministry as a whole.

With this background in mind, the contrast between the working of the planning and budgeting procedures in the two countries becomes plain. In the United Kingdom, the guidance to the Service departments, which undertake the detailed work of preparing the budget, will have been thoroughly discussed throughout the ministry as a whole. The guidance should be sufficiently precise to enable the Service departments to make satisfactory plans within their budget limits. In the United States, guidance coming from the Office of the Secretary of Defense (OSD) is so general that, as General Jones and others have pointed out, it demands more forces than the budget will allow. The Services are therefore able to fix their own priorities instead of having to work to a set of priorities laid down by the Defense Secretary after receiving military advice. Mr. McNamara's difficulties in attempting to ensure a common procurement policy by the US Navy and US Air Force for the TFX (later F111) show the problems that can ensue when a solution (correct or incorrect) has to be imposed by the Office of the Secretary of Defense on the Service departments.[10]

A HYPOTHETICAL CASE

To take this comparison a little further, it will be helpful to consider a hypothetical problem in the field of conventional war and see how each system would handle it. Suppose that each nation was considering a large purchase of tactical aircraft to support the land forces primarily in an antiarmour role against attack by a sophisticated opponent, in other words to support NATO forces in Central Europe. It would be highly desirable, particularly if there was severe financial stringency, to compare the effectiveness of a purchase of aircraft for the Air Force under consideration with the expenditure of the same sum on additional tanks or antitank weapons (including helicopters) for the Army. It would also follow that analysis should enable those faced with a decision on resource allocation to establish the best mix of ground-based and airborne weapons for this task. This hypothetical example might involve the transfer of financial resources from one Service to another in an area that each Service would regard as sensitive and not to be relinquished.

A US Secretary of Defense, if faced with this problem, would certainly have to include mention of it in the Defense Guidance, that is the budgetary and planning guidance issued by his office when the annual budget is being prepared. One may suppose that the guidance of the Secretary of Defense would indicate that a certain sum of money was being set aside either for aircraft or for Army weapons and would direct that both the Army and the Air Force should prepare analyses of the effectiveness of their proposed weapon purchase in an antiarmour role for submission to the Secretary of Defense for a final decision. At this stage, the program analysis and evaluation (PA&E) divisions of the two Service departments would presumably prepare analyses to show that the purchase of the weapon by their own Service would result (in any future European war) in the destruction of more enemy armour at lower cost than could be achieved by the alternative proposal. When these analyses had been forwarded by the two Service departments to the Office of the Secretary of Defense, the PA&E staff there would have the unhappy task of advising the Secretary of Defense on a solution to this problem.

It would be naive to suppose that the analysis produced by such adversary proceedings (to use again the phrase of the Blue Ribbon Defense Panel) would dovetail neatly and suggest a solution. It is also unlikely that the PA&E staff in the Office of the Secretary of Defense, however experienced or expert, could produce a detailed analysis of the air-ground interaction in relation to the antitank problem that both the Services concerned would accept. No doubt, the Defense Resources Board under the Deputy Secretary of Defense would be asked to advise on the problem, but it is hard to see them providing an agreed solution.[11] Nor are there many outside agencies or research organisations with both the standing and the expertise to achieve the same result.

The majority of the outside institutions are too closely tied by contractual obligations to one Service to be accepted by the other Services as impartial when vital Service interests are affected. The Institute for Defence Analyses, which does work under contract for the Joint Chiefs of Staff (JCS), might undertake work of this sort, but this institute could find great difficulty in producing results acceptable to both Services, particularly since the abolition of the Weapons System Evaluation Group in the mid–1970s. This situation would probably involve the Joint Chiefs of Staff in an embarassing decision when that body would be asked to endorse a decision that would be highly unpopular with one of the two Services concerned. General Jones' recent criticisms of the JCS organisation (see chapter 4) would appear to support this view of how events might unfold.

In short, the Secretary of Defense would probably not receive one comprehensive analysis of the situation that could command either respect or assent from both the Services concerned. He would find it hard to obtain unbiased neutral advice about the trade-off problem that he had posed, let alone persuade others of its rightness. Of course, even if this advice could lead him to the correct answer, he might feel it necessary to accede to bureaucratic pressures and choose another solution that left each of the adversary Services at least partially satisfied. But whatever the constraints imposed by the internal politics of the department, the organisation and procedures of the department should be capable of producing impartial analysis and advice for the Secretary of Defense even if the complexity of the problem precludes advice that is so complete and final as to persuade all those involved of its logic and correctness.

The Department of Defense fails to produce such analysis for problems of conventional war for two reasons. First, any attempt to use the tight framework of annual budgets to settle a major problem of the type suggested creates unnecessary difficulties by shortening time for discussion and by posing the dilemma in the acute form of robbing Peter to pay Paul; and yet in a sense this is the only opportunity the Secretary of Defense has to achieve results because his main means of controlling Service expenditure is the annual defence budget. The second and equally important reason is that the organisation of the Department of Defense has not encouraged the growth of an impartial analytical capability, shared by the three Services on a continuing basis, for the study of conventional war. The Program Analysis and Evaluation Office (PA&E) of the department is unable to fulfill this role as neutral analyst and arbiter for a number of reasons, some of which derive from the hostility with which it was viewed during the McNamara era. At present, therefore, it is hard to see a PA&E study involving a major reallocation of the defence budget being accepted by the Service department concerned. The same considerations would apply to any outside agency or "think tank" presented with problems in this area; it is unlikely that any of them could be effective without a large additional staff of active-duty officers from all three Services with recent experience of the types of weapons under discussion in combat or at least in peacetime operational conditions.

Finally, it may be argued that the procedure suggested for the solution of this hypothetical problem is unreal and unnecessarily tips the scales against the achievement by the US Department of Defense of a logical solution. There is some justice in this argument, although the procedure suggested is based on that laid down by Mr. Schlesinger in 1974 and parallels, particularly in the role suggested for the Office of the Secretary of Defense, can be found both in the Thor/Jupiter controversy and in the discussions preceding the decision on the TFX (F111). But even if the procedure is regarded as a simplified version, a skeleton as it were, of a more elaborate procedure probably extending over several years, the shape of the skeleton is basically correct. The main outlines of the adversary procedure suggested here would almost certainly apply in the United States.

How would the British Ministry of Defence resolve a similar problem? A very different process would be involved, and because this is the home of Defence by Discussion it would entail, as one would expect, a network of committees. The first and major difference from the US system is that the guidance issued for the long-term costings should not, when dealing with a problem of this complexity, create a debate between adversaries for resolution at a later stage. It is far more likely that the original proposal for additional tactical aircraft would be processed in the same way as would any proposal for the procurement of a major weapon system. This process must therefore be briefly described.

Two committees are successively involved in a major procurement proposal: first, the Operational Requirements Committee (ORC) and second the Defence Equipment Policy Committee (DEPC). The ORC, under the chairmanship of the Deputy Chief of the Defence Staff with representatives of the Permanent Under-Secretary and Defence Scientific Adviser as full members, reports to the Chiefs of Staff Committee; ORC will give an agreed view on the operational needs that the new weapons systems must meet. This committee is likely to be a forum in which the professional military viewpoint will receive every consideration and possibly be dominant. The DEPC, under the chairmanship of the Chief Scientific Adviser, has as full members the Service representatives of the Procurement Executive, as well as civilian representatives of the Permanent Under-Secretary. This is the forum in which the Service department concerned puts its case for the particular weapon system that, in its view, meets the operational need endorsed by the ORC. The ORC must endorse the operational need for a weapon, and the DEPC must confirm that it can be produced at an acceptable cost within a reasonable time. When these approvals have been obtained, major proposals must be submitted to the Secretary of State and the Treasury. If delays occur or the cost escalates, then the project must go back to the DEPC for further approval. Of course, the DEPC and other committees have the continuing task of ensuring that a project once approved is not unduly delayed, is kept within reasonable cost limits, and remains technically capable of meeting the need for which it is designed. The problems involved in that task are not relevant to the present issue, which is to describe how a contentious proposal gets over the ORC and DEPC hurdles for the first time.[12]

From the start, the Defence Secretariat, the defence scientific staffs, and the defence operational requirements staff would have been aware of and involved in the problem being used as an example. The two Service departments concerned would therefore have had frequent contacts with those who were hostile to or doubtful of their proposals and who would be sitting on either or both of the committees through which the proposals must pass. Moreover, to quote Michael Howard on the subject of weapons procurement, "the necessary links between technical, military, financial, and political considerations are not hammered out in the committees but forged and kept forged by telephone calls, informal meetings, and massive circulation of memoranda between the military and civil officials to whom the process comes so naturally that they find it difficult to explain exactly how it is done."[13]

At some stage during this process, analysis of the cost effectiveness of the two options would be called for. This analysis would almost certainly be done by, or in conjunction with, the Defence Operational Analysis Establishment (DOAE) at West Byfleet, which has developed an impressive array of models representing land-air warfare in the central region of Allied Command Europe. Here, if they are given the time to study the particular problem, the staff should be able to offer advice that stands a reasonable chance of being acceptable to the Service departments concerned because a number of officers from each of the Services with relevant experience will have been involved in all stages of the analysis both in the ministry and at DOAE West Byfleet.

This is a brief sketch of how the UK system for selecting the most effective weapons systems should work, particularly if the House of Commons Defence Committee's 1982 proposals for increasing the role of DOAE are implemented.[14] Provided that sufficient time was available, the Secretary of State for Defence should have before him an impartial analysis of the effectiveness of two alternatives on which to base his decision. This analysis should have involved all those with a direct interest in the final decision and would have evolved gradually as a collective effort. Therefore, the Secretary of State need not judge between two sets of arguments produced by competing adversaries. This process, if it works, is Defence by Discussion. Perhaps the picture painted is idealised, but it is based on existing organisation and procedures and can be made to work in this way given sufficient encouragement from the top.

This is not, of course, to imply that the Secretary of State can ignore the pressures of bureaucratic politics, and he may finally decide that he cannot accept the "rational" solution since he must accommodate pressures either from within the department or from within the government, or indeed from elsewhere in the NATO alliance. He may therefore decide on a compromise solution that satisfies, to some extent at least, those who cannot be convinced. But, it is worth repeating, this outcome does not imply the failure of the analysts whose advice has not been taken. Those responsible for the organisation of defence policymaking must devise one to produce impartial advice and to warn the decisionmaker of the problems involved in accepting it. Rational policymaking is the proper objective of an organisation, but to describe an organisation only in these terms may not necessarily provide a convincing explanation of what actually happens. It would not be right to give the impression that the organisation always works in this ideal way, but to repeat, it is designed to work rationally, and given the will of those at the top, can be made to do so.

CONCLUSION

The hypothetical example suggests that those charged with making defence policy ought to have comprehensive and impartial analysis of the defence policy options open to them. But unless they are prepared to ride roughshod over the important components of the organisation for which they are responsible, then this analysis must be acceptable to the Service adversely affected by the decision. If one of the Services rejects the analysis on which a defence policy decision is based, then historical precedents in both the United States and the United Kingdom show that the Service will attempt to delay or otherwise thwart the implementation of the decision while seeking to get it reversed.

It was surely these considerations that led Mr. Laird to institute participatory management of the defence budget,[15] but as has been seen, this change did not solve the problem. As former Department of Defense official Ronald Fox wrote, "four years after the institution of participatory management, it is clear that decentralization has meant a return to military hard-sell. The Services are reemphasising the practice of reducing ongoing program budgets in order to free funds for new programs, disregarding the effect of Service-centered planning on the efficiency of overall defense planning and funding."[16] By accepting a diminished status and authority for the analytical capability directly responsible to him, Mr. Laird had in consequence to face "the threat that US force levels could again come to resemble those of the 1950s, reflecting the interest of three separate Services and not corresponding to coherent overall defense planning."[17] This is not to suggest that the authority and status of the Office of the Secretary of Defense as a whole suffered a decline similar to that experienced by Program Analysis and Evaluation, but, except possibly during the Carter administration, succeeding Secretaries of Defense have not apparently used systems analysis as a means of directly influencing the resource allocation process.

There are no indications that this trend has been reversed. General Jones' criticisms in 1982 would indicate the contrary. Whatever changes have taken place, the comparison with the United Kingdom is instructive. Implicit in Defence by Discussion is the assumption that impartial analysis of all options is built into the system. All Secretaries of State for Defence who take charge of a Ministry of Defence based on the 1964 reorganisation have an analytical capability in the defence policy staff, and the related Defence Secretariat and defence scientific staff that can command a large measure of support from the ministry as a whole. This analytical capability is part of the structure of the organisation and relies for its continued effectiveness not so much on the views and wishes of the Secretary of State at the time, but on its own authority and influence with the rest of the ministry.

Chapter Twelve

Some Possible Solutions

Before sketching in the elements of an ideal defence organisation, it is worth examining some of the proposals for diminishing inter-Service rivalry that have been put forward but not completely adopted in the past.

One way of solving the problem, which has proved popular with Prime Ministers and Presidents in the past, has been to cut down the size of the Defence Minister's opponents at the council table; namely, the Service ministers. This solution has been frequently adopted in the United Kingdom with the result that the three political appointments in charge of the Service departments have been downgraded three times since 1960, and in 1981 the parliamentary under-secretary posts in charge of the three Service departments were abolished and two new posts of the same rank were created: one with responsibility for administration of the three Services and the other for equipment.

In the United States, the Service Secretaries have, as a result of the same process, lost cabinet status and much of their prestige and power. Despite these changes, the single Services are still powerful. In the United Kingdom, this power is concentrated in the three Service Boards—committees of senior officers and civilians with collective responsibility for the administration of their Service. Their deliberations are presided over by one of the five politically appointed ministers, but this hardly weakens the single-Service flavour. In the United States, the independence of the three single Services is protected by the 1947 National Security Act and its successors; power lies with the Chief of Staff, the professional head of Service, and the civilian Service Secretary. Downgrading has not so far solved the problem of inter-Service rivalry in either country.

FUNCTIONALISATION

If further progress were to be made in reducing the power of the Service departments, it would probably be necessary to "functionalise" the whole Defence Department. Under this solution, the headquarters would be divided into sectors dealing with defence policy, personnel, logistics, procurement, and so forth, on a tri-Service basis. This solution has had powerful and experienced advocates in the United Kingdom. Both Lord Mountbatten and the authors of the Ismay-Jacob report favoured functionalisation[1] and saw the 1964 reorganisation as one step on the way toward the complete functionalisation of the ministry and the disappearance of the Service departments as separate entities. It is true that a number of important tasks in the British Ministry of Defence are dealt with on a defence-wide basis, including accounting, audit, personnel management of civilians, contracts, computers, and the administration of lands, but the essential basis of the ministry is still the Centre (the central policy planning and budget staffs) and the three Service departments. Funtionalisation has been less of an issue in the United States, perhaps because the independence of the Service departments is entrenched by the 1947 National Security Act and its successors. In view of the support that it has received, the case for complete functionalisation must be answered.

Before reaching a view on functionalisation, one must decide what a ministry (or department) of defence should do. In both democracies, Great Britain and the United States, with freely elected legislatures, the ministry is first and foremost a department of state through which the elected government issues instructions to the armed forces of the nation. Equally, the armed forces must make known their requirements for funds, legislation, and so forth, through this department. It is also an operational headquarters, turning the government's decisions and policies into operational plans and orders for the forces. It also plans the defence budget over the long term (the form of defence policymaking that is the subject of this study). Finally, the ministry must be the administrative headquarters, organising the personnel, logistic, and procurement requirements of the three Services. It is not essential that defence departments carry out all these tasks, but they do in both the United Kingdom and the United States.

When these tasks are set down together, the end product of the organisation, namely, the three Services in the field, receives proper notice. In both the United States and the United Kingdom, the armed forces and their supporting civilian establishments are by many criteria the largest and most complex organisations in the nation. Moreover, one of their prime and continuing tasks is the maintenance at operational readiness of comparatively large forces to protect their nation against attack. Any nation with potentially hostile forces ranged against it would be well advised not to risk the upheaval of reorganising on functional lines without carefully examining the alternatives.

Moreover, a defence organisation must be able to react to the unexpected and mount operations for which no previous plans exist. These requirements put a premium on good organisation. One aspect of this was the need faced by the United Kingdom on at least two occasions in the last ten years to cut defence expenditure sharply and quickly. As has already been noted,[2] it is normally left to the Service departments to survey their reduced resources and propose the least damaging economies. The central policy staffs can suggest which international or strategic commitments should be dropped but have no means of costing or even describing the savings in depots, weapons, or men that might result. Another example of the unexpected was the mounting of the Falkland Islands campaign by British forces in 1982; this campaign involved sending land, sea, and air forces over 8,000 miles to fight battles for which no contingency plans existed. These examples are given not to support an argument for no change in the organisation in case operational readiness is affected, but to stress that one essential end product of a Ministry of Defence is the ability to project force in a sudden or unforeseen crisis.

If defence ministers and others wish to reorganise, and therefore disrupt for some period, an organisation capable of these complex administrative tasks, they would no doubt look for examples of major industrial organisations, with a wide spread of activities, that organise themselves on functional lines. Suitable examples are hard to find. Received managerial wisdom appears to be to give maximum power to the factory manager, and to the extent that this is not possible, power should go to a group headquarters controlling subunits with similar end products. This lack of precedent may not be the most compelling argument for avoiding the functional solution, but the absence of precedents outside the defence world is certainly remarkable.

The extreme, "green," solution adopted by the Canadian government is relevant. In the mid-1960s, the Canadian Army, Navy, and Air Force were replaced by a single, unified armed service with a green uniform, and the Canadian Ministry of Defence was functionalised. There is still dispute over the success of this reorganisation. Little in the way of dramatic savings or revolutionary decisions are now attributed directly to the reorganisation, which is often the case. Probably the total size of Canada's armed forces (about 80,000) is small enough to allow a headquarters organised on functional lines to work effectively. It is unlikely to work for the United Kingdom (about 340,000 servicemen) or the United States (some two million in the armed forces).

If, as appears to be the case, the existing organisations are efficient means of operating and administering the end products of defence, namely, the Services, then defence managers and defence planners should be required to produce stronger arguments for a functional organisation of defence. Otherwise, the proposal will look suspiciously like another move in the process of reducing or disorganising one's opponents instead of winning the argument by rational methods. Surely it would be better to adopt other and less drastic methods of improving the planning organisation before resorting to the functional solution.

THE OKW SOLUTION

Another drastic possibility, the "OKW solution" should be mentioned. The Oberkommando der Wehrmacht (OKW) was responsible to Hitler during World War II for all the German armed forces. The OKW solution would involve establishing a large tri-Service planning headquarters separate from the Ministry of Defence and interposed between the ministry and the armed forces. This idea was hotly discussed, or rather argued against, in the United Kingdom during the years preceding the 1964 reorganisation by those who said that any further weakening of the Service departments would lead to a situation in which the central defence staff would grow greatly in size and come to resemble the OKW in Germany between 1939 and 1945. According to these critics, OKW had immense powers to plan operations, but no responsibility for carrying them out. In consequence, so the argument goes, the German armed forces were set impossible tasks and lost the war.

However, as Michael Howard has pointed out, "the analogy with the OKW was and remains curiously inept."[3] Research has shown that OKW was responsible for planning some successful campaigns and had no part at all in a number of Germany's major military failures between 1939 and 1945. It seems likely that the creation of unified Ministries of Defence with integrated defence planning staffs will, in future, avoid the need to have large unified joint Service headquarters interposed, like OKW, between the government and the Services. The concept of a unified Ministry of Defence in which both planners and those in charge of operations are responsible to the senior Service officer in the department should bridge the gap between power (the planners) and responsibility (the operational commands). Certainly, President Eisenhower's decision in 1958 to remove the Service departments from the operational chain of command has not had the disastrous effects that those opposing a divorce between power and responsibility would no doubt have predicted. Although the Joint Staff and, thus, in effect the US Joint Chiefs of Staff do have oversight of operational commands, the gap between planning and administration is in the US system quite considerable.

HOW MANY SERVICES?

Finally, for the sake of completeness, two courses of action occasionally suggested as a solution to the problem of inter-Service rivalry (and much else) must be mentioned. There are those who feel many defence problems would be eased if the number of Services were reduced from three to two (not counting Marine forces). The Air Force is usually, if not always, selected for the "chop" in this solution, perhaps on the grounds that it is the newest and that the United Kingdom won one World War and the United States two without its separate help. It should be clear from the previous discussion that this proposition has nothing to commend it in this context (or probably in any other). Quite apart from denying the supreme flexibility of air power, the reduction in the number of claimants for scarce defence resources does not simplify any of the most difficult decisions on allocation (for example, between strategic and conventional forces) and ignores the extremely complex administrative tasks that have persuaded most of those who considered the possibility of functionalising the UK Defence Department itself to reject that solution as administratively dangerous.

A more logical variant of the three-into-two solution is mentioned and dismissed by John Ries.[4] This solution would entail the "functional development of the Services into a few highly specialized commands (such as strategic, limited war, and home defense)." The initial attraction of the proposal is, of course, that Service missions would be brought into harmony with the nature of the weapons systems—strategic, tactical, and defensive—thus precluding inter-Service argument about alternative methods of carrying out any mission. For Professor Ries, writing in 1964, the overwhelming disadvantage was that by abolishing the incentive for the Services to find better and cheaper ways of carrying out missions assigned to other Services, one lost the benefit of inter-Service competition, which was the "surest and cheapest insurance that can be purchased against a future gap in defense capabilities." This argument does not sound quite so attractive almost twenty years later, but he is surely right to stress that the solution ignores the distinction between the problems of the application of force and those connected with resource allocation to create force. Even if resource allocation problems were to be eased by reorganising the armed forces in this way, there is no promise at all that command and control in war, particularly in operations for which no previous plans existed, will be simplified or improved. As with the functionalisation solution discussed earlier in this chapter, the proposal might ease resource allocation problems at the probable cost of immensely complicating the problem of using the forces once they have been created.

If then dramatic solutions are not available to cut the "Gordian Knot" of defence (dis)organisation, the next step must be to consider some of the key elements of the ideal defence organisation that the experts might recommend for, say, Ruritania (wherever that country is).

Chapter Thirteen
The Essentials of a Defence Organisation

> It should be borne in mind that there is nothing more difficult to arrange, more doubtful of success, and more dangerous to carry through than initiating changes in a state's constitution. The innovator makes enemies of all those who prospered under the old order, and only lukewarm support is forthcoming from those who would prosper under the new. Their support is lukewarm partly from fear of their adversaries, who have the existing laws on their side, and partly because men are generally incredulous, never really trusting new things unless they have tested them by experience.[1]

Machiavelli is quite right, of course, and no attempt will be made in this study to prescribe changes in either the US or UK defence organisation. Perhaps, however, some general points for further study can be discovered from the extensive comparisons that have been made. There should be enough material to try to discover the essential elements of an ideal defence organisation. Because Utopia is not threatened by war, this ideal will be designated as the Ruritanian Ministry of Defence. Ruritania is situated in Europe, has land frontiers with powerful neighbours, a sea coast, and possessions in the Pacific. It has an Army, Navy, and Air Force, each sufficiently large to preclude the dominance of any one Service. They are, therefore, equal contenders in the share out of the defence budget. Ruritania's Minister of Defence has, in consequence, the same problem as his colleagues in the United States and the United Kingdom, namely, how to get three Armed Services of approximately equal status and power to settle on a coherent defence policy with a rational distribution of limited defence funds, instead of allowing each to bargain to maximise the benefits for, or minimise the damage to, their own Service.

If, following the discussion in previous chapters, the need for separate Service departments, each responsible for all the administration, support, and training of its own Service, is accepted, then the second essential ingredient in the ideal defence organisation is surely a strong central defence policy staff. This staff should report to the senior Service officer in the ministry with the responsibility for advising the government on defence policy and be similar to the staff introduced in the United Kingdom in 1982, and proposed by General Jones, US Air Force, at about the same time.

In one way or another, the supreme Service authority must be required to give advice on what is best as a defence policy rather than try to achieve the best compromise between the three Service positions. It is therefore essential that the officer concerned should have joint staff responsible directly to him, and this staff should be organised so that each planning team's responsibilities are matched as closely as possible to the likely commitments of the forces for which they plan. Thus the US or UK teams dealing with the land-air battle in Europe should comprise only soldiers and airmen experienced in that theatre and, as planners, should be exclusively concerned with it. Similarly, the possible outcome of a maritime battle in the North Atlantic should be the responsibility of a team composed of sailors and airmen only. If Ruritania considers the main threat to be a land invasion from Freedonia, she would be well advised to concentrate one planning team exclusively on that threat. No doubt, some minor tasks will not warrant the full-time attention of a planning team, but as far as possible those commitments or threats calling for significant shares of the defence budget should warrant a planning team to deal with them. The exact relationship of the Service members of these planning teams to their own Service and its Chief of Staff is a matter on which the Ruritanian Defence Minister should listen very closely to his single-Service Chiefs of Staff. However, he must grasp the nettle and ensure that the joint planners have an overriding responsibility to the Chairman of the Joint Chiefs of Staff (or Chief of the Defence Staff). The planning staffs of the Services must also be prepared to play an active and crucial role in the resource allocation process.

These planning groups must be well supported by scientific staff able to conduct analyses of weapon effectiveness and to devise models to simulate conflict involving more than one Service; in other words, these analysts must be prepared to work across inter-Service boundaries. The Defence Ministry's central financial and budget staff must be so organised that they can be closely associated with each planning group. The constraint of limited resources for defence must be uppermost in the minds of all defence planners, analysts, and financial staff.

The next item on any list of requirements is surely obvious, even if controversial. If the defence planning staff and all those engaged in defence policymaking are to be organised by function or program, then the defence budget must be organised in the same way. For planning purposes only, the budget must be reorganised along the lines envisaged by the PPB system or the UK functional costings. However, one important change is required.

The functions, programs, or outputs, must be chosen so that all the items included in each function contribute toward the objective of that function, with the cost of multifunction forces and weapons shared between the functions. Thus, one obvious function or program category for UK and US budgets would be general purpose forces in Europe. Under this heading would be included all forces, land and air, active duty or reserve, whose task in war would be to engage in, or support, battle with Warsaw Pact forces on the European continent. The maritime general purpose forces assigned to the North Atlantic should form a separate program category. It is true that the results of any conflict with Soviet naval forces in the Atlantic would in due course affect fighting in Europe, but the conflict would be a separate one, and possibilities exist for tradeoffs between the relevant sea and air forces because all are committed for one purpose: maritime conflict, mainly in the Atlantic.

Table 9.1 shows the existing major programs in the US defence budget and the UK counterpart known as the functional analysis of the defence budget, as well as a possible structure for a Ruritanian defence budget. This structure should also be suitable with some modification for US and UK defence planners. There are admittedly great difficulties in dividing up the whole defence budget so that all or nearly all of it is attributed to end products, such as strategic or theatre land and air forces. Some research and development, intelligence, communications, and defence headquarters costs will no doubt have to remain as residual items, but the aim should be to allocate all possible support costs to the frontline forces requiring them. In this way, the planners responsible for optimising the effectiveness of any function or program will have the maximum freedom to consider costed options and tradeoffs realistically.

Some supporters of the PPB system may well feel that what is proposed does not go far enough. If the programs or functions of the budget must be so self-contained that all the items in any program must contribute to the same precise objective, then how can those at the highest level decide how to share out the budget between major programs. On this argument, one of their hardest tasks is, for example, to justify the resources devoted to strategic nuclear forces in view of the pressing needs for extra conventional forces. The new system will give no help at all on this or similar problems (for example, Can Ruritania afford a nuclear deterrent? Should it have a Navy able to defend its isolated possessions in the South Pacific?). These problems must be accepted. No doubt, incremental decisionmaking (in the sense of starting with current tasks and commitments and considering the effect of marginal increases or decreases in resources) will help, but the PPB system and systems analysis cannot answer these questions by quantitative analysis alone. These techniques succeeded in clarifying the answer to the question, "How much is enough strategic deterrence?" because they identified the resources that all three Services were devoting to the task (which was to be capable of eliminating a set proportion of the population and the industry of the Soviet Union) and showed up the "flat of the curve" where extra resources devoted to the set objectives would have a sharply diminishing effect. But none of the techniques available showed what level of destruction would deter, nor whether the United Kingdom or Ruritania needed a nuclear deterrent at all. Nevertheless, the role for analysis within each of the programs will be immense.

These proposals should also escape the axe of those convinced opponents of the PPB system, such as Aaron Wildavsky who wrote, "PPB fails because no organisational level gets information (1) that it is willing to use and (2) that is relevant to the resources at its disposal."[2] Under the system now proposed, the PPBS programs and the planning teams will be organised in identical lines and the cost of each program category will define precisely the resources at their disposal for planning purposes.

Another objection will perhaps come from Naval and Air Force officers, who could argue that it is quite wrong to tie to one theatre or task such versatile weapons as ships or aircraft which can be deployed from one threatre to another. Aircraft in particular could possibly in a NATO conflict be moved from the European land battle to the Atlantic sea battle in time to influence the results in both. This objection misunderstands the nature of analysis and planning. There are two levels of optimisation. At the operational level, the commanders in charge at the time must use what is available in the most effective way. At the planning level, those with the task of making the best use of limited resources cannot exempt from scrutiny such versatile weapons systems as, for example, strike aircraft which can be amongst the most expensive in the inventory (as an example, the UK Tornado programme was in 1982 expected to cost $18 billion, compared to $10 billion for Trident). When, as with the Tornado, the plane can be deployed in several modes and in several theatres, the division of costs between programs or functions will no doubt cause much discussion, but the cost advantages of multirole aircraft will surely persuade the planning teams to agree on a division. These calculations, like those involved in assessing the total costs of a future weapon system, must inevitably be approximate. This approach is reasonable, provided there is no attempt to fudge doubts and uncertainties, because this is an exercise in future planning, not an attempt to attribute actual costs when these are incurred.

This link between future projections and actual costs brings to mind another possible objection. Those concerned with the audit of expenditure, management accounting, or financial control could argue that their tasks will be impossible if all accounting is to be in terms of functions, programs, or outputs. This objection is to misunderstand what is proposed. When the ministry has settled each year how the defence budget is to be divided between outputs, it can then redivide the same sum in terms of inputs (such as men, weapons, and buildings, which have to be bought in that year). Both US and UK defence budgets are recast this way at present to satisfy congressional and parliamentary requirements. It may perhaps be unfortunate that the two legislatures require costs to be submitted in this way, but so long as they do, the costs of defence can be recast without requiring the planners and Chiefs of Staff to stop thinking in terms of force levels and weapons programmes.

If Ruritania follows the advice given so far, her central defence planning and policy staffs will have a voice in budget and procurement decisions. At that stage, these staffs will surely ask for some assurance about the long term so they can make firm commitments and enable the Services to negotiate between themselves the timing of the introduction of new weapons systems. In support of their request for a system of multiyear budgeting, the planners would no doubt point to the advantages of the British PES system and some of the reports of the US Congressional Budget Office, notably the 1977 report on *Advance Budgeting*.[3] But from the planners' own point of view, perhaps the simplest analogy gives the most convincing argument.

Anyone building a house on limited space would be wise to draw a plan first to ensure that everything can be fitted in. Similarly, defence planners, seeing the need for very expensive weapons programmes for all three Services stretching over a number of years, will inevitably have to tailor and time these programmes so that the cost peaks in each do not all occur in the same year and swamp the likely defence budget. For this task they need as much certainty as possible about future defence budgets. Long-term financial planning has another significant advantage already noted—it facilitates inter-Service agreement on the timing and size of weapons programmes. Any Service will be less reluctant to forgo the chance to start a major weapons programme, if the Service is confident that it can introduce the programme within the next two or three years with the agreement of the other two Services. This ability to negotiate over time is a key part of Defence by Discussion.

Critics of multiyear budgeting, such as Aaron Wildavsky, will no doubt be sceptical of any system of long-term financing. In 1979, he pointed out that the British PES system, which he aptly describes "as a pact between central controllers and spending departments to sustain mutual stability," had become "a shambles," because "rampaging inflation running into the high twenties, coupled with low rates of economic growth, led to vast increases in expenditure without offsetting additions to revenue." As a result, "PES has been trimmed to three years with the last two years' expenditures left vague and placed on a cash (current price) basis."[4] This criticism of the PES system applies, of course, to government expenditure as a whole. It has much force, particularly as it applies to revenue forecasts, and stresses the extent to which government spending must depend on the prosperity of the country. However, as far as British defence planners are concerned, the PES process described in chapter 9 still fulfills an essential purpose. Just as the Public Expenditure Survey as a whole was a pact between Controllers and spenders for their mutual benefit, so within defence the long-term planning associated with the PES system is part of a pact between the Services to avoid a last-minute scramble each year for money for new projects. If the participants can believe in a system of multiyear budgeting, it can work.

However, UK planners are not so naive as to believe that expenditure for year ten or year five will inevitably turn out as it was originally planned. They are well aware of the electoral process and realise that a government of a different political complexion will not necessarily feel itself committed to all the defence decisions of its predecessor. They also realise, however, that weapons programmes have a momentum of their own: if the orders are placed overseas, there may be heavy cancellation charges; if they are to be produced at home, the financial disruption and unemployment involved in their cancellation will also be unwelcome to the government in power. In this uncertain area, defence planners would surely be right to concentrate on the next three to four years, building as much certainty into that period as they can by seeking government commitments to future weapons systems. The change to cash planning in the PES system, therefore, has not necessarily altered the realities of long-term planning within the Ministry of Defence. The final years of the ten-year programme were never really credible, but did provide a useful framework for tentative agreements. Attention has always concentrated on the early years, and cash planning merely reinforces this tendency.

Because the Ruritanian constitution (like that of the United States) shares the power of the purse between the executive and legislative branches, instead of concentrating it in the hands of the government and its majority in the legislature (as in the United Kingdom), it is less easy for the Ruritanian Ministry of Defence to make long-term plans with confidence. Much can, however, be accomplished if, as in the United States, the legislature is prepared to grant obligational authority for major weapons programmes at the start of production. Although this action does not commit Congress to any level of spending either on defence as a whole or on any particular weapon system in any one year, the Department of Defense has implicit authority for a core of future defence budgets. This authority allows some planning for the future but not enough for the ideal defence organisation because those planning future weapons programmes that have the backing of the President of the day cannot be certain that

Congress will consent to them. Perhaps the Ruritanian legislature would consider one change in their current procedures for controlling expenditure. If they were prepared to agree with the Ruritanian President and his executive on a joint resolution setting total defence expenditure for each of the next three or four years (on lines suggested in 1983 to President Reagan and Congress by the Bipartisan Appeal, as described at the end of chapter 9), then they could eliminate many of the disadvantages of year-to-year budgeting.

Many critics will be unconvinced, arguing perhaps that defence planners by the nature of their work must seek to map out the future even though electoral changes or national economic misfortunes could render their plans no better than castles in the sand. Two replies are possible. First, a long-term financial plan for defence embodies the expected consequences of present decisions. The correct reaction to the unexpected is to alter the plan, not to scrap it. Second, in the context of Defence by Discussion, a plan will have much validity for the future if a fair proportion of those responsible for the plan are available when the time comes to change it. In particular, agreements reached between the Services on the need for, and phasing of, future weapons programmes may well hold in changed circumstances if the participants are part of a cohesive group with a tradition of continuous service and mutual trust. This observation brings us to the final element in the ideal defence organisation.

As the previous paragraphs have implied, a permanent nucleus of planning and budgetary staff is needed to provide a continuing oversight of the long-term plan. It is highly desirable that Service officers should stay three or four years in important defence policy posts—even longer tours would be helpful, but four years is probably about the limit if they are to retain up-to-date experience of the operation of their Service. Whitehall or Washington warriors skilled in bureaucratic infighting through long service in the corridors of power, but not responsive to the real needs of their Service, are not a satisfactory substitute for the career civil servant.

Chapter 8 mentioned some of the advantages that two American observers of the Whitehall scene saw in the British system of career civil servants. The creation of the Senior Executive Service provided an opportunity to improve the position of full-career civil servants in the United States, but if defence planning is to be effective, one more step is needed. It is not enough for senior civil servants to remain in the civil service after a change of government; they should, if administration is to be effective, be expected to remain in the same post (whilst being able to move at other times to other civil service jobs to gain experience). The regulations of the US Senior Executive Service do not guarantee this continuity of position or even assume it as a matter of course. The permanent cadre of staff should also reach to the top echelons of the ministry, excluding only the small number of political appointees needed to oversee the activities of the ministry. If Ruritania is able to adopt such a solution, she will obtain both administrative advantages through greater continuity and some assurance that her Ministry of Defence will be able to take a long-term view.

Two aspects of this proposition will probably evoke dissent from American readers. They will say first that five "political" or presidentially appointed posts is far too small a number to control a large, modern defence department; and that if a newly elected administration is to be confident of carrying out its own policies, it must reach down at least three layers into the bureaucracy (to assistant secretary in US and deputy secretary in UK terms), and perhaps more, to place its own appointees in the 80 to 120 key positions where they can gather the information and make the subordinate decisions necessary to effect major policy changes. They will also argue that if it is necessary in Ruritania or elsewhere to provide opportunities for a fuller career in senior positions to improve the quality of the permanent civil service, then this result can be achieved by the creation of something on the lines of the US Senior Executive Service, which provides for continuity of employment and possibly of grade but not of position after a presidential election.

The exact number of political appointees in a ministry is clearly a matter for discussion, taking account of the detailed circumstances. The decision should take account of the disadvantages of discontinuity near the top and the countervailing advantages of previous experience when new policies are planned. Professor Heclo calculated in 1977 that twenty-one months was the average length of tour of those holding under secretary and assistant secretary posts throughout the US government.[5] Even if one accepts that matters have improved since then, or were never as bad in the Department of Defense, an average tour of two years for the top civilian echelons in defence has some disturbing implications. Few, if any, of those at the highest level who were responsible for planning expenditure before any fiscal year will be available after that year is complete to answer questions about actual expenditures from Congress, auditors, and others. It also means that, on the reasonable assumption of at least two years relative stability between major defence policy reviews, very few if any senior civilians will remain in post from one defence review to the next.

The difficulties of the novice administrator in Washington have been well rehearsed by Heclo and others and need no repetition here.[6] One advantage of continuity needs restressing. If inter-Service rivalry is to be diminished and a coherent defence policy is to emerge, there is a clear need to take the longer view, to conduct discussion in terms of functions or program categories that may well be unfamiliar to the newcomer (whether he is a political appointee or service officer), and to draw upon the results of past discussions and analyses of relevant, but perhaps distantly related, issues. All these are proper tasks for career civil servants, either administrators or scientists, who can tap the corporate skills and experience of colleagues in a way a newcomer could not emulate. British, French, and German experience, to cite only three examples, would endorse the value of the career bureaucrat in such circumstances.

It is often suggested that the bureaucracy of senior career civil servants in relatively permanent positions of power provides an almost insuperable obstacle to change. Much ink has been spilled and a television comedy series created on this subject.[7] Those who complain of an all-powerful British civil service tend to ignore the fact that the promotion of civil servants to the most senior appointments is controlled by the government of the day;[8] but most observers would surely accept that defence is a special case. The bureaucracy engaged in defence planning and policymaking must contain a very high proportion of Service officers on tours of three, or in some cases, four years. They should bring with them recent experience and new ideas. Whatever preconceptions or prejudices that Service training may produce, they are unlikely to be those acquired by a permanent civilian bureaucracy. In any case, it should not be assumed that the scientific advisers and analysts in defence institutions, whatever their previous experience, are likely to share any prejudices bred into their administrative counterparts. In short then, the picture of a monolithic bureaucracy, deeply entrenched in its own prejudices and totally resistant to change, is not one that is easily applied to a department of defence, and there is no reason to reject the concept of a permanent civilian bureaucracy on this account.

From the foregoing, therefore, it becomes clear that a coherent, effective defence organisation would have the following characteristics:

Strong administrative departments for each Armed Service;

A powerful central policy and planning staff (with Service officers and civilian administrators and scientists) to plan defence policy, the budget, and weapons projects;

A planning, programming, and budgeting system with functional categories or programs directly related to the specific tasks of the armed forces;

A long-term or multiyear budget system to provide as stable an environment as possible for future plans; and,

A full-career civilian bureaucracy of administrators and scientists to operate this system in equal partnership with their Service colleagues.

These are the essentials of a defence organisation and Ruritania would be well advised to adopt as many of these as she can. One more ingredient is needed: a well-informed sector of public opinion based on academic and specialist institutions with a close and informed interest in defence matters—but this sector cannot be created overnight by those reorganising departments of defence.

Afterword: Defence Reorganisation 1984

[*Author's note:* Michael Heseltine, Secretary of State for Defence, announced his plans for a further reorganisation of the Ministry of Defence when this book was being printed. The publishers agreed to include the Secretary of State's paper as an Annex to the book, together with my own brief comments, which are as follows.]

The Heseltine reorganisation, which has not been worked out in detail, relies on two well-tried methods of containing inter-Service rivalry. The first is to increase the power of the central defence staff. On this occasion this is to be achieved by integrating into it the civilian staff dealing with policy and by making CDS and PUS jointly responsible for the integrated staff. This may in time create the ideal impartial defence staff envisaged in the 1963 White Paper but much will depend on how the new staff is to be organised. Some of the options suggested in paragraph 17 of the paper resemble those proposed in Chapter 13 of this book for the ideal defence organisation; but there is no mention of the need to reshape the defence budget also mentioned in that chapter.

The second method used in the past to try to ensure that the defence view prevailed was to weaken the power of the Service Departments. Mr Heseltine has made shrewd use of this approach. By abolishing the Vice Chiefs of Staff in the three Services together with the operational and planning staffs reporting to them, he has removed the obvious focuses for the formulation of single Service points of view on major issues of resource allocation. Many of the single Service operational and planning staffs will no doubt reappear in the reorganised defence staffs, but the departure of the Vice Chiefs of Staff deprives the Services of one of their best placed spokesmen in inter-Service discussions on defence policy.

It is still too early to discuss the other changes announced or foreshadowed in the paper. The subordination of the Chief Scientific Adviser to the PUS recognises that the third member of the triumvirate had not the same powers as his two colleagues CDS and PUS; but it is doubtful whether either the United States or the United Kingdom has yet found a satisfactory way of incorporating defence analysis into the budget process. The analyst must aim to be relevant and at the same time keep himself immune from short term problems—never an easy combination. The creation of an Office of Management and Budget will apparently involve no new tasks for finance and budget staffs but is designed to ensure closer control by the Centre. Much will depend on how finance staff is to be deployed at lower levels and the extent to which future Secretaries of State will be prepared to operate with less detailed financial control (which is entailed in the new scheme for responsibility budgets referred to in paragraph 20 of the paper) when, as has happened on previous occasions, increased financial delegation leads to some financial laxity at the periphery.

Finally, there is the problem of the Service Boards. They are to be retained but the Secretary of State's paper emphasises that the Executive Committees of the Boards will be responsible, in the first instance, for the administration of their Services; it also stresses that they will not be asked to offer advice on policy. Evidently the status of the Boards is to be diminished and they are to be discouraged from formulating single Service views on defence policy. The aim is understandable in the light of past experience but there are dangers if debate on major issues is to be confined to the defence staff. Competition between the US Services has on occasion encouraged innovation and increased efficiency. Unless the UK's major single Service Commands at home and overseas can assume responsibility for what the paper describes as the 'operational' and 'policy' functions of their Service, Britain's defence planners may in future defence reviews fail to consider some important options for the better allocation of defence resources.

Annex: MINIS and the Development of the Organisation for Defence

(Paper by the Secretary of State for Defence, Defence Open Government Document 84/03)

(1) This paper is about management structures. That is a matter of central significance but it cannot be allowed to detract from the critical emphasis we must always place on the front line readiness and capability of our Armed Forces, and our ability to support them.

(2) The Defence Budget has risen significantly, reflecting the very high priority given to defence by the Government. The budget is nonetheless under pressure from the growing demands for resources generated by the impact of new technology and advances in the threat. It is of paramount importance that those responsible for the management of defence ensure that the benefits of additional resources are applied to enhance the fighting effectiveness of our Armed Forces. We must not prejudice the support of the front line, but there is no place for unnecessary bureaucratic or manpower intensive overheads. This key part of our responsibilities, and the best possible reassurance to the key part of our responsibilities, and the best possilbe reassurance to the public—who bear the cost of defence—of our proper and wise stewardship of the resources provided.

(3) Nowhere is this more important than in the Ministry of Defence itself. During the last twelve months I have been involved in the examination of the MOD through the MINIS process. I have looked in some detail at the workings of key staffs, and in particular at organisational problems—many of which have been evident since the very early days of the Ministry. I indicated not long after my appointment my wish to consider further whether the present federal form of higher defence organisation is still right in today's circumstances. Now after a year of operating MINIS in MOD I am convinced from what I have seen that:

(a) The organisation is less economical than it should be, particularly in senior posts, in the use of deputies, and in narrow spans of command;
(b) Too many lines of accountability are blurred;
(c) The process of giving advice and taking decisions too often reflects compromise.

(4) I believe that the time has come to move forward and to simplify radically the present structure with the objective of cutting overheads, both directly through reducing the size of the staffs involved and indirectly by removing impediments to improved accountability, more delegation and the more efficient use of resources. I wish therefore to open a period of discussion and consultation, leading by the Summer to the detailed working out of proposals for change. I shall put these detailed plans to my colleagues, and it is my intention to present them subsequently to Parliament.

(5) My starting point is that the identities of the three separate Armed Services must be retained. As the 1963 White Paper (*Central Organisation for Defence*, Cmnd. 2097) put it, 'the fighting spirit of the individual man in battle derives largely from his loyalty to his ship, his unit or his squadron'. There can be no question of my determination to uphold these loyalties and traditions, that have stood so well the test of time and combat.

(6) The constitutional position of the Defence Council and the Service Boards is unchanged. Within the Ministry itself, however, I wish to draw a clearer distinction between:

(a) The formation of advice on operations, defence policy, and resource allocation—which are central to the Ministry; and
(b) the management of the Services themselves which I have already said I wish to see decentralised as far as practicable outside MOD, progressively under a regime of responsibility budgets.

(7) Oversight of the management of each Service should in my view be the principle concern of the Service Chiefs of Staff. In particular, I envisage that they should continue to be responsible for the total efficiency and morale of their Services. In future, however, I wish them to report through CDS to me for that purpose.

(8) More specifically, the management functions in relation to Service personnel, training, logistics and supply should be exercised through *Executive Committees*, as sub-committees of the Service Boards, chaired by the Chief of Staff, in accordance with policy directives laid down by the central staffs, and within centrally determined budgets for each of the main expenditure programmes of the Executive Committee members. These Executive Committees would have an important role—but one concerned with administration not policy, as indeed was the original intention of the 1963 White Paper in respect of the Service Boards themselves.

(9) In addition to the Service Chief of Staff, who would act as Chairman, the membership of the Executive Committee might appropriately include the Principal Personnel Officer and Principal Administrative Officer for the Service concerned, the appropriate Systems Controller, and the 2nd PUS.

(10) When the unified MOD was created in 1964, it was envisaged that there would be substantial rationalisation of personnel and logistic functions—to a greater extent than has, I believe, actually occurred, although there have been worthwhile advances over the last 20 years. I take an essentially pragmatic view of the scope for further rationalisation between the Services, but I need to be satisfied that the personnel and logistic functions are being administered with the maximum efficiency and that opportunities for economy are seized with vigour. If this means further rationalisation, then it must take place.

(11) An early task for each Executive Committee would be to draw up a programme of work aimed at streamlining management in their area, including further delegation of authority for day to day administration where possible to Commanders-in-Chief, and reducing the potential overlap that exists between headquarters P&L staffs and those of Commands. There could be advantage in Commanders-in-Chief or their senior officers being invited to attend meetings on occasion. Consideration may well also have to be given to changes in some areas of the Command structure itself to allow clear and unequivocal devolution of authority.

(12) Turning to *policy and operations* matters, I wish to be assisted in future by a *Defence Staff* charged with, in the words of the 1963 White Paper, 'the corporate duty of finding the best defence solution to the problems of the day, whether of an operational nature, strategic planning, defence policy or equipment priorities'.

(13) The recent changes designed to strengthen the position of the CDS, whilst vaulable in themselves, have served to accentuate the organisational separation of his Central Staffs from the Naval, General and Air Staffs in a way which I believe was never intended by the architects of the Ministry. The time has come to recognise the interdependence of the subjects with which they deal and to bring the relevant Staffs of DCDS and the single-Service Vice Chiefs together.

(14) I have seen both in MINIS and in day to day work how closely and well the civilian Secretariats under the DUS(Policy) and the Staff

AUSs work with the uniformed Staffs. I believe that efficiency in administration would be greatly improved if this close working was recognised organisationally by bringing the DUS(P) and his Central Staffs, and those Staff Secretariats dealing with the political aspects of defence policy and operations, into the central organisation, thus creating *a fully unified and integrated military/civilian Defence Policy and Operational Staff*.

(15) This unified and integrated Defence Staff would provide advice for all parts of the Ministry, including as appropriate the Service Chiefs of Staff and members of their Executive Committees, covering:

- (a) future defence requirements, in the light of the developing military threat, and in terms of the UKs commitments and long-term concepts of operations;
- (b) military priorities in the allocation of resources (including personnel) between and within Service programmes; and the detailed operational requirements for equipment;
- (c) joint and single-Service plans for operational deployments by the Services, and instructions for the conduct of operations and exercises;
- (d) defence intelligence relevant to the exercise of these responsibilities;
- (e) political and parliamentary aspects of the work, and its coordination with the FCO and other government departments.

(16) I see the Chiefs of Staff Committee continuing, with its present membership. It would be supported by the Defence Staff. But it would be CDS who would in future be responsible for the preparation for and conduct of all military operations and not just as at present those involving more than one Service. The necessary operational directives and instructions would therefore be issued by the Defence Staff on the authority of CDS. Responsibility for the advice given by the Defence Staff generally would rest with CDS and PUS jointly or severally as appropriate—command and professional military advice on operations resting for example with CDS as principal military adviser to the Government, and relations with other Government Departments resting with PUS. Most of the specific responsibilities of the Service Vice-Chiefs would therefore pass to the new Defence Staff and their present posts would lapse. The main coordinating responsibilities of the VCDS(P&L) would also fall to the Defence Staff, and I would envisage that the post in its present form—including its membership of the Defence Council—would lapse.

(17) The internal organisation of the Defence Staff would have to be that best fitted to its defence-wide function, and would incorporate the relevant elements of the present Naval, General and Air Staffs. Detailed plans for the organisation and its complement will have to be worked out, but several options for the basic structure are discernible, for example:

(a) A broad split between 'policy and programme' work and 'commitments' (including coordination of operations) as exists at present in DCDS's staff, with staffs grouped accordingly;
(b) A functional split of the work, by geographical area/commitment (e.g. Home Base, Atlantic, Central Region and 'rest of the world'), or by military capability (e.g. sea/air, land/air, nuclear and further sub-divisions).

(18) I can see that there is in theory a third option, of 'single-Service' groupings of staff, responsible for all the 'operational' and 'policy' functions of that Service, but working within a single framework and under higher-level direction. I should make clear my own view that such an alternative would be likely to mean the continuance of separate Central, Naval, General and Air staffs in a new guise; that the savings in top posts would be fewer; and that common solutions to defence problems would be reached less efficiently. But I do see the Defence Staff, however structured, being constituted of single-Service building blocks—and there will of course be a need for detailed study of the level at which they are aggregated. I also assume that it would be desirable, under any option, to preserve the separate identity of the Defence Intelligence Staff (and, indeed, of the Defence Signal Staff).

(19) Within the options in paragraph 16 above, there would be scope for considerable variation in the details including the deployment of the civilian officials who will have an important role to play. I should make clear however that I believe that substantial savings can be made in top posts and lower down the structure of the new Defence Staff.

(20) The third area in which fundamental change is needed is in *resource allocation and finance*. I have laid down elsewhere the way ahead which I see for improved management through a system of responsibility budgets of different types. The corollary of such a system is much stronger central determination of priorities and control of resource allocations, down to the level of Service sub-programmes (ie covering the expenditure of individual Board members). By 'control' I mean a process of budget setting, agreement to forward programmes to

match, and monitoring of performance, and audit. The 1963 White Paper placed responsibility for long-term financial planning and control of the defence programme and the allocation of resources on the Permanent Secretary, supported by the Defence Secretariat. This central responsibility seems to have been dissipated through the system of target headings, with the 'Service Departments', both civilian and uniformed, becoming more involved in the allocation of resources at the macro-level than was originally foreseen or in my view subsequently justified.

(21) I believe that the best way forward is to concentrate responsibility for finance and budget, resource allocation and audit matters in an '*Office of Management and Budget*', as a central organ of the Ministry, responsible to PUS. I intend that 2nd PUS should be Controller-General of this Office of Management and Budget, and that he should direct the work of the staffs of the Principal Finance Officer, the Principal Establishments Officer and DUS(PL), together with the 'size and shape' Defence Secretariats. I shall expect reductions in the number of senior civilian posts as a result.

(22) The primary objective of the Office of Management and Budget (OMB) would be to achieve stronger control over the MOD's corporate planning, the commitment of resources, and the financial and management systems which the department follows throughout its work. I want to be able to turn to a 'Finance Director' who can assure me that he is satisfied with the advice given on financial and management matters, or the decisions taken on his behalf by staff with clear and unequivocal lines of reporting to him. This need not imply any greater centralisation of decision-taking, but 'delegated powers', whether to staffs in the P&L areas, in the PE, or to line management 'in the field' need to be clearly spelt out and performance monitored. The vital linkage with the management level would be achieved by 2nd PUS's membership, as Controller-General of the OMB, of each Service Executive Committee.

(23) The OMB would be responsible for issuing the assumptions for the Service programmes for the Long Term Costings in accordance with the policy priorities advised by the Defence Staff, and for coordinating the resulting costing. The OMB would agree proposals for budgets for major sub-programmes managed by Board members, and would scrutinise on behalf of Ministers and the Accounting Officers new requirements for major equipment and projects. The existence of the Combined Defence Staff will to a large extent sweep up the work of the current Operational Requirements Committee chaired by DCDS, since

the combined staffs will be working on operational requirements in a single organisation, albeit in close consultation with the staffs of the OMB and the PE. Advice on the affordability of major projects would rest with the OMB, taking advice from the Defence Staff and PE, and consulting Ministers as necessary. (Advice on production proposals could, however, continue to come from the PE as now.) There may well be a continuing need for a single high-level equipment committee on the lines of the present Defence Equipment Policy Committee, but I should like the question of Chairmanship to be further considered.

(24) To sum up, my proposed changes involve therefore three essential elements:

(a) the Service Chiefs of Staff will be responsible to me through CDS for the efficiency and morale of their Services, and they will chair the Executive Committees which, under the Boards, will oversee the management of the Services;
(b) formulation of policy, operational, military and political advice by a Combined Defence Staff, which will incorporate both the relevant elements of the Naval, General, Air and Central Defence Staffs, and civilian staff from the relevant Secretariat Divisions;
(c) allocation of resources and coordination of financial management by an Office of Management and Budget under the 2nd PUS, responsible to the Permanent Secretary.

Within this framework there is, of course, scope for pursuing a number of different options for the detailed allocation of responsibilities, on which further study will be needed before taking my ideas further.

(25) Changes are also needed elsewhere in the Ministry. The Controller, R&D Establishments Research and Nuclear is already considering proposals for a streamlining of the *Service Chief Scientist/ Directors General of Research area*. I should now like the Chief Scientific Adviser to work with CERN to produce joint proposals, including the centralisation of the 'scientific adviser' functions under CSA. This would entail central management of operational analysis work currently carried out by the 3 Service Chief Scientists who would in future report to CSA. I should like to emphasise the importance I attach to a small but strong scientific staff within the Ministry to provide an independent capability for original thinking on long term strategic options, and on the roles and equipment of the Services. I believe that this capability is best provided to the Services from a centrally run staff.

(26) I attach great importance to the possibilities of realistic and verifiable *arms control*. I wish in future to be advised by a central Defence Arms Control Unit including both professional military and civilian advisers, responsible jointly to CDS and PUS but organisationally separate from the Defence Staff.

(27) Changes are also needed to the *procurement of defence equipment*. I am discussing this with the National Defence Industries Council and the matter can be pursued independently of the present proposals for the remainder of the Ministry. But I shall wish to look subsequently at the organisation of the Procurement Executive, and indeed the whole arrangements for defence material. Mr Levene is also investigating on my behalf other problem areas, such as the Royal Dockyards.

(28) Overall, the changes I have outlined would lead to a considerable simplification of the existing structure. I attach importance to the organisation reflecting the realites of power and responsibility—I do not like finding, as I have done too often in MINIS 1, significant differences between working practices and the formal structure. I have set out at Appendix A therefore a chart showing how I see the higher organisation for defence in future. This reflects my view that I should have two principal advisers, CDS and PUS. I do not rule out any member of the Defence Council submitting his views to me, or to my Ministers, concerning his area of responsibility, but the essential structure of the Ministry should be that shown in Appendix A. As the single Service Chief of Staff will report to me through CDS, so the Chief Scientific Adviser and the Chief of Defence Procurement will be responsible to me through PUS.

(29) Throughout the MINIS 1 process I have not sought to hide my view that fundamental change is needed in the Department's organisation. I am clear that change on the lines I have indicated is both feasible and necessary, and that significant savings in senior posts both Service and civilian can and must be achieved. I have not produced detailed plans and it would have been wrong for me to try to do so without the benefit of consultation. This outline will need to be translated into a detailed, tightly complemented organisation, with proper spans of control and without unnecessary deputies.

(30) That radical change is afoot is not something we should seek to conceal from the public, Parliament, or the staff of the Ministry. But it is in the interest of all that we should keep the period of speculation to a minimum. I welcome therefore the opportunity of opening this period

of consultation which I hope will lead quickly to agreement on the detailed blueprint for the future higher organisation for defence.

Ministry of Defence
March 1984

Envoy

London and Washington

Of course, there can be no firm conclusions to a comparative study like this one. Chapter 13 may suggest some lines of enquiry, but the quotation from Machiavelli preceding it reminds us that politicians must spend much time and political capital, both scarce commodities, if they wish to reorganise any government institution, and the time is rarely ripe for this activity.

If change is to come to defence, it should come from the inside. An organisation is composed of rational men. They should be able to agree to changes that help them to do their job better. They will agree more readily if informed outsiders, encouraged perhaps by the specialist committees in Parliament and Congress, were to discuss the problem and suggest improvements. The debates on this change will have to start in London and Washington, cities as different as chalk and cheese.

As many have remarked, Washington is a company town and the name of that company is government. It is a city open to outsiders and receptive to new ideas. Few in Washington will refuse to discuss the problems of government, and it is always possible to find someone who knows personally the expert on any subject. In this sense, it is a tight little city, but so close to government that its newspapers are sometimes less critical of government than are their counterparts in, say, New York.

London is different. The heart of London is the City, the centre of finance and commerce, sheltered behind mediaeval walls that have not quite disappeared. London is cautious and critical of government but not really interested in its problems. Government is expected to get on with its job and to make any necessary changes in the bureaucracy without bothering Londoners. Closed government makes for swift changes, but the lack of open debate hinders informed discussion on what these changes should be. Conversely, in Washington much debate can be expected on matters such as defence reorganisation, but desirable changes may have to be forced through against vocal opposition.

What a pity that each city cannot borrow the good points of the other! But if they did, each would lose its own flavour—so perhaps they are best left as they are.

Notes

Chapter One

1. *Public Papers of Presidents of the USA, Harry Truman, 1945* (Washington, DC: US Government Printing Office, 1961), p. 551.

2. The phrase "the three Armed Services" will recur frequently in this book. If Marine forces are counted as a separate Service, then the reference should be to four Armed Services.

3. J. Garnett, "Constraints on Defence Policymakers," in *The Management of Defence,* ed. L. Martin (London: 1976), p. 40.

4. P. Y. Hammond, "Super Carriers and B36 Bombers: Appropriations, Strategy, and Politics," in *American Civil-Military Decisions,* ed. H. Stein (Birmingham, AL: 1963).

5. Quoted in B. Reed and G. Williams, *Denis Healey* (London: 1972), p. 199.

6. V. Davis, *The Admirals' Lobby* (Raleigh, NC: 1967).

7. J. D. Steinbruner, *The Cybernetic Theory of Decision* (Princeton, NJ: 1974), p. 72.

8. In an advertisement in the *New York Times* on 6 April 1983, the Bipartisan Appeal suggested to President Reagan a number of areas of possible duplication or redundancy, including strategic bombers and missiles and tactical air support for the Army. They also questioned whether sea-based air attacks on Soviet ports was a worthwhile mission. Other possible areas of waste through inter-Service rivalry will be discussed in later chapters. Chapter 9 discusses the Bipartisan Appeal's proposals for long-term budgeting.

9. K. Waltz, *Foreign Policy and Democratic Politics* (London: 1968); R. Burt, *Defence Budgeting: The British and American Cases* (London: 1975); and see also relevant articles in *The Defense Policies of Nations,* eds. D. J. Murray and Paul R. Viotti (Baltimore, MD: 1982).

10. J. M. Roherty, *Defense Policy Formation* (Columbia, SC: 1980), p. 4.

11. Richard E. Neustadt, *Alliance Politics* (New York: 1970), p. 139.

12. M. Halperin, *Bureaucratic Politics and Foreign Policy* (Washington, DC: 1974). This topic is discussed more fully in chapter 5.

Chapter Two

1. See P. Blau, *Bureaucracy in Modern Society* (New York: 1956), for an extended treatment of Weber's ideas.

2. See especially J. March and H. Simon, *Organisations* (New York: 1958), and R. M. Cyert and J. March, *Behavioral Theory of the Firm* (Englewood Cliffs, NJ: 1963).

3. C. I. Barnard, *The Functions of the Executive* (Cambridge, MA: 1938), pp. 185–86.

4. J. Garnett, "Constraints on Defence Policymakers" in *The Management of Defence*, ed. L. Martin (London 1976), p. 30.

5. R. Bauer and K. Gergen, eds., *A Theory of Policy Formation* (New York: 1968), p. 5.

6. R. M. Cyert and C. N. March, *A Behavioral Theory of the Firm* (Englewood Cliffs, NJ: 1963), chap. 6, p. 118.

7. See J. D. Steinbruner, *The Cybernetic Theory of Decision* (Princeton, NJ: 1974), pp. 71–78, for a fuller treatment with examples, one of which has been quoted in chap. 1.

8. H. J. Leavitt, *Managerial Psychology*, 3rd. ed. (Chicago, IL: 1972), chap. 24.

9. J. Dawson, "An American View of Defence Management," in *The Management of Defence*, ed. L. Martin (London: 1976), p. 48.

10. G. T. Allison, "Conceptual Models and the Cuban Missile Crisis," in *Comparative Foreign Policy*, ed. W. F. Hanrieder (New York: 1971), p. 362.

11. C. Lindblom, "The Science of Muddling Through," *Public Administration Review* 19 (1959): 79–88. For a full development of the contrary view, see C. Schultze, *The Politics and Economics of Public Spending* (Washington, DC: 1968). The latter contains a valuable reminder that Lindblom's well-articlulated theories should not be compressed and over simplified. This author's defence is that he is merely attempting to set a limit to the application of theory with which Professor Lindblom might well agree; see Schultze, op. cit., p. 37.

12. C. Lindblom, *The Intelligence of Democracy* (New York: 1965), passim.

13. A. Wildavsky, *The Politics of the Budgetary Process*, 3rd ed. (Boston, MA: 1979), p. 148.

14. R. Sanders, *The Politics of Defense Analysis* (New York: 1973), p. 11.

15. H. J. Leavitt, *Managerial Psychology*, pp. 281–82.

16. The cybernetic theory of decisionmaking accepts that this complexity exists but argues that, as Robert Coulam puts it, "decisionmakers act routinely on the basis of simplified images of complex problems, oblivious to their effect except insofar as the simplifications themselves are affected." See R. F. Coulam, *Illusions of Choice* (Princeton, NJ: 1977), p. 17. Coulam's theory is persuasive and is not basically at variance with the arguments put forward in this study for the greater use of analyses in defence resource allocation.

Chapter Three

1. W. F. Monypenny and G. E. Buckle, *Life of Benjamin Disraeli*, vol. 4 (London: 1910–20), chap. 2, p. 37.

2. *Royal Commission into the Civil and Professional Administration of Naval and Military Departments*, C5979 (London: 1890).

3. M. Howard, *Central Organisation for Defence* (London: 1970), p. 5.

4. See: L. W. Martin, "The Market for Strategic Ideas in Britain: The 'Sandys' Era," *American Political Science Review* 56 (March 1962): 23–26. Others have described this era as Defence by Committee; see especially F. Johnson, *Defence by Committee* (London: 1960).

5. *Defence Estimates 1956–57* (London: 1956).

6. H. Macmillan, *Tides of Fortune* (London: 1969), p. 560, column 396.

7. House of Commons Official Report, 24 January 1957.

8. F. Johnson, *Defence by Committee*, p. 344.

9. C. J. Bartlett, *The Long Retreat* (London: 1972), p. 129.

10. R. N. Rosecrance, *Defence of the Realm* (London: 1968), pp. 239–42.

11. M. Howard, *Central Organisation for Defence*, p. 10.

12. See L. W. Martin, "The Market for Strategic Ideas in Britain: The 'Sandys' Era," p. 31.

13. M. Howard, *Central Organisation for Defence*, p. 11.

14. Ibid.

15. Ibid.

16. Ibid., p. 15. This topic is discussed further in chap. 12.

17. *Central Organisation for Defence*, Cmnd 2097 (London: 1963).

18. G. Williams and B. Reed, *Denis Healey* (London: 1971), chap. 8.

19. Ibid., p. 203.

20. *Second Report of the Defence Committee of the House of Commons 1981–82*, vol. 2 (London: 1982), p. 502.

21. Lt. Gen. Sir Maurice Johnston, "More Power to the Centre: MOD Reorganisation," *RUSI Journal* (March 1983).

22. Although the title Defence Policy Staff is no longer current, it will be used, with or without capital letters, elsewhere in this book because this title gives a better description for the layman of the task that the staff perform.

23. R. Hastie Smith, "The Tin Wedding," in Seaford House Papers (London: 1974), p. 35.

24. See D. Greenwood, *Budgeting for Defence* (London: 1972), especially chap. 3, for a fuller description of this process; also see R. Burt, *Defence Budgeting: The British and American Cases* (London: 1975).

25. R. Hastie Smith, "The Tin Wedding," p. 36.

26. D. Greenwood, *Budgeting for Defence,* p. 41

27. The 1981 Defence Review, which culminated in the Defence White Paper CMD 8288, was handled in this way.

28. M. Howard, *Central Organisation for Defence,* p. 7.

Chapter Four

1. See P. Hammond, *Organizing for Defense* (Princeton: 1961), chap. 8, and D. Caraley, *The Politics of Military Unification* (New York: 1966), passim.

2. This remark by President Eisenhower was quoted in the *Report of the Blue Ribbon Defense Panel* (Washington, DC: 1970), p. 14.

3. R. Albion and R. Connery, *Forrestal and the Navy* (New York: 1962), pp. 280–81.

4. P. Hammond, *Organizing for Defense,* pp. 234–36.

5. US, Senate, Armed Services Committee, *National Security Act Amendments, Hearings,* 81st Cong., 1st sess., 1949, p. 9.

6. *Report of the Blue Ribbon Defense Panel,* p. 14.

7. H. S. Truman, *Memoirs,* vol. 2, *years of Trial and Hope* (London: 1956), p. 64.

8. See especially *The Report of the Rockefeller Committee on Department of Defense Organization* (Washington, DC. 1953).

9. J. M. Roherty, *Decisions of Robert S. McNamara* (Miami, FL: 1970), chap. 1.

10. *Report of the Blue Ribbon Defense Panel,* p. 15.

11. US, Senate, Subcommittee on National Policy Machinery, *Hearings* (Washington, DC: 1961), vol. 1, p. 769.

12. J. M. Roherty, *Decisions of Robert S. McNamara,* p. 66.

13. C. J. Hitch, *Decisionmaking for Defense* (Berkeley, CA: 1965), p. 18 et seq.

14. Ibid., p. 34.

15. Terminology in this field can play havoc with the uninitiated, especially the British reader who has learned that systems analysis is an essential preliminary to programming work for a computer. See chapter 10, this book, and R. Sanders, *Politics of Defense Analysis* (New York: 1973), chap. 1, for a fuller explanation of these definitions.

16. A. Enthoven and B. Smith, *How Much is Enough?* (New York: 1971), pp. 172–84.

17. J. M. Roherty, *Decisions of Robert S. McNamara*, p. 70.

18. *Report of the Blue Ribbon Defense Panel* (Washington, DC: 1970), p. ii.

19. See I. F. Stone, *Polemics and Prophecies* 1967–70 (New York: 1970), p. 170.

20. M. Laird, *United States Military Posture for FY 1971* (Washington, DC: 1970), p. 8.

21. R. Sanders, *Politics of Defense Analysis*, p. 97.

22. M. Halperin, "The President and the Military," *Foreign Affairs* (January 1972).

.23. *Report of the Blue Ribbon Defense Panel*, p. 21.

24. This statement is based on interviews held in the United States in 1975. It would be interesting to speculate what changes Mr. Richardson might have made since he has the reputation in Washington of being an outstanding administrator.

25. *Report of Secretary of Defense James R. Schlesinger to the Congress on the FY 1975 Budget* (Washington, DC: 1974), p. 217.

26. See especially his chap. 6, "Planning for Planning," in *Planning US Security*, ed. Philip S. Kronenberg (Washington, DC: 1981).

27. President Carter's reluctance to initiate reforms in the Department of Defense, despite the good advice that he had received, may well have been due to the increasing hostility he faced from the congressional committees dealing with the Armed Services.

28. The initiatives taken by Mr. Carlucci, Deputy Secretary of Defense 1980–82, were important, but did not directly affect resource allocation procedures, being more concerned with achieving realistic cost estimates, decentralising and reforming weapons procurement, and improving control of costs. They did, however, involve greater delegation of budget responsibilities to the Service departments and increasing the size of the Defense Review Board.

29. This article was reprinted in *Armed Forces Journal International*, March 1982. The most convenient source for General Jones' views is his evidence to the US, Congress, House, Investigations Subcommittee of the Committee on Armed Services, 97th Cong., 2d sess. (HASC no. 97–41).

Chapter Five

1. M. Halperin, *Bureaucratic Politics and Foreign Policy* (Washington, DC: 1974), p. 104.

2. See H. Heclo and A. Wildavsky, *The Private Government of Public Money* (London: 1973) p. 141.

3. G. Williams and B. Reed, *Denis Healey* (London: 1971), p. 196.

4. L. W. Martin, "The Market for Strategic Ideas in Britain: The Sandys' Era," *American Political Science Review* 56 (March 1962): 23.

5. R. Hofstadter, *The American Political Tradition* (New York: 1957), p. 8.

6. M. Taylor, *The Uncertain Trumpet* (New York: 1959), p. 78.

7. H. S. Truman, *Memoirs,* vol. 2 (London: 1956), p. 64.

8. S. E. Finer, *Comparative Government,* Pelican ed. (London: 1974), p. 252.

9. M. Halperin, *Bureaucratic Politics and Foreign Policy* (Washington, DC: 1974),. chaps. 1, 16.

10. See P. F. Brundage, *The Bureau of the Budget* (New York: 1970), p. 140 et seq., for a fuller description.

11. L. Legere, "Defence Spending: A Presidential Perspective," *Foreign Policy* (Spring 1972): 93.

12. M. Halperin, *Bureaucratic Politics and Foreign Policy,* p. 231.

13. D. D. Eisenhower, *The White House Years,* vol. 2 (New York: 1965), p. 713.

Chapter Six

1. S. E. Finer, *Comparative Government* Pelican ed. (London: 1974), p. 176.

2. House of Commons, Select Committee on Procedure, *Scrutiny of Public Expenditure and Administration*, Cmd 410 (London: 1969), p. v-xviii.

3. M. Howard, "Civil-Military Relations in Great Britain and USA, 1945–1958," *Political Science Quarterly* (March 1960).

4. P. F. Brundage, *The Bureau of the Budget* (New York: 1970), p. 140.

5. S. Huntington, "Strategic Planning and the Political Process," *Foreign Affairs* (1960): 287.

6. But see Priscilla Clapp "US Domestic Politics and Relations with Japan" in *United States-Japanese Relations in the 1970s.* eds. P. Clapp and M. Halperin (Cambridge, MA: 1974), p. 46, for a more up-to-date assessment that broadly supports Huntington.

7. L. A. Dexter, "Congressmen and the Making of Military Policy" in *Components of Defence Policy*, ed. D. B. Bobrow (Chicago, IL: 1965), p. 95.

8. M. Halperin, *Bureaucratic Politics and Foreign Policy* (Washington, DC: 1974), p. 258.

9. L. Radway, *Foreign Policy and National Defense* (Glenview, IL: 1969) p. 109.

10. Ibid., p. 109.

11. D. Caraley, *The Politics of Military Unification* (New York: 1966), p. 189–90.

12. Ibid.

13. M. Halperin, *Bureaucratic Politics and Foreign Policy*, p. 256.

14. K. Waltz, *Foreign Policy and Democratic Politics* (London: 1968).

15. D. Caraley, *The Politics of Military Unification*, p. 207 et seq.

16. Notably by S. E. Finer, *Comparative Government*, Pelican ed. (London: 1974), p. 249.

17. D. Caraley, *The Politics of Military Unification*, p. 143.

Chapter Seven

1. S. E. Finer, *Comparative Government*, Pelican ed. (London: 1974), p. 63.

2. This was not so in earlier times. See Brian Bond, "Outsiders Influence on Defence Policy," *RUSI Journal* (March 1982).

3. L. W. Martin, "The Market for Strategic Ideas in Britain: The 'Sandys' Era," *American Political Science Review* 56 (March 1962): 32.

4. House of Commons, *Official Report*, 11 November 1959 cols. 378 et seq.

5. D. D. Eisenhower, *Memoirs*, vol. 1, *Mandate for Change* (New York: 1963), p. 347.

6. D. Halberstam, *The Best and the Brightest* (London: 1972), pp. 174–75.

7. L. Radway, *Foreign Policy and National Defense* (Glenview, IL: 1969), p. 13.

8. For an example of this, see M. Armacost, *The Politics of Weapon Innovation* (New York: 1969), pp. 124–28, which describes the Nickerson incident in which a US Army colonel was reprimanded for his over-zealous advocacy of strategic nuclear weapons for the Army.

9. S. Brown, *The Faces of Power* (New York: 1968), pp. 172–73.

10. *Common Cause* (October 1982).

11. *New York Times*, 7 November 1982.

12. C. P. Snow, *Science and Government* (Cambridge, MA: 1960), p. 1.

13. Ibid., pp. 56–66.

14. Much of this, notably A. Wohlstetter's essay "Strategy and the Natural Scientist," in *Scientists and National Policymaking*, eds. R. Gilpin and C. Wright (New York: 1964), pp. 174 - 239 is not relevant to this study.

15. M. Armacost, *The Politics of Weapon Innovation*, p. 252.

Chapter Eight

1. See chapter 4 note 29.

2. P. Appleby, "An American View of the British Experience," in *The Public Service and University Education,* ed. J. McLean (Princeton, NJ: 1949), p. 180.

3. "Senior civil servant" is defined for the purpose of this study as being those in the UK grades of assistant secretary and above. This definition is dictated by the convenience of the comparison of these grades with the supergrades of the US civil service. It includes scientists as well as administrators and the figures quoted relate to March 1983.

4. See especially chap. 3, H. Heclo and A. Wildavsky, *The Private Government of Public Money* (London: 1973).

5. D. Halberstam, *The Best and the Brightest* (London: 1972), p. 38.

6. The nearest parallel might be Milner's *'Young Men' in South Africa 1901–04.*

7. The figures and statements in this and the preceding paragraphs are based on information obtained at interviews in the Department of Defense in March 1983, and from information supplied by the UK Ministry of Defence at about the same time.

8. I am indebted to Professor Hugh Heclo for permission to quote from an article of his, which is now published in *Bureaucrats and Politics: A Comparative Study,* ed. E. Suleiman (New York: 1983).

9. M. W. Huddleston, "The Carter Civil Service Reforms," *Political Science Quarterly* (Winter 1981–82).

10. T. B. Clark, "Senior Executive Service—Reform from the Top" *National Journal* (30 September 1978).

11. W. J. Languette, "SES from Civil Service Showpiece to Incipient Failure in Two Years," *National Journal* (18 July 1981).

12. Comparisons are not easy, but between 1974 and 1983 the number of senior noncareer civilian staff appears to have increased marginally over that period. Information about retirement of senior staff was obtained at interviews in the Department of Defense in March 1983.

13. A fuller description of one such process in the Ministry of Defence is given in chapter 11, this book.

14. R. Morriss, *Haig, The General's Progress* (Los Angeles, CA: 1982), p. 67.

Chapter Nine

1. E. R. May, *Treatise on the Law, Privileges, Proceedings, and Usage of Parliament,* 17th ed. (London: 1964), p. 715.

2. See A. Schick, *Congress and Money* (Washington, DC: 1980), especially p. 357 et seq.

3. A. Enthoven and W. Smith, *How Much is Enough?* (New York: 1971), p. 33.

4. Report to Senator Kennedy from the Committee on the Defense Establishment, 5 December 1960.

5. J. Kraft, "McNamara and His Enemies," *Harpers Magazine* (1961): 42.

6. A Schick, "A Death in the Bureaucracy," *Public Administration Review* (March 1973).

7. Ibid.

8. A. Wildavsky has dealt trenchantly with the value of PPBS in budgeting; see especially chap. 6 of the third ed. of his *The Politics of the Budgetary Process* (Boston, MA: 1979). His conclusions are discussed further in chapter 13 of this book.

9. A. Schick, "A Death in the Bureaucracy," p. 152.

10. The Department of Defense has made great efforts to solve this problem of combining the stability of the program elements with the flexibility to re-sort and reaggregate them into different displays as analysts perceive new requirements. But the various mission-oriented resource displays, etc., are not published and cannot therefore form the basis of useful public debates. The best solution still seems to be to restructure the basic elements in the way suggested in this study.

11. See especially D. Greenwood, *Budgeting for Defence* (London: 1972), passim.

12. *Report of the Committee on the Control of Public Expenditure,* CMD 1431 (London: 1961).

13. *First Report from the Expenditure Committee, 1975–76,* CMD611 (London: 1975.)

14. R. Sanders, *The Politics of Defense Analysis* (New York: 1974) p. 84.

15. See especially *Time* (27 December 1982).

16. US, Congressional Budget Office, *Advance Budgeting: A Report to Congress* (Washington, DC: 1977). See also A Schick, *Congress and Money* (Washington, DC: 1980), p. 142.

17. "A Bipartisan Appeal for a steady, coherent, and affordable multiyear defense buildup," *New York Times,* 6 April 1983, pp. A12–13.

Chapter Ten

1. This was briefly discussed in chapter 2, this book, but see Ralph Sanders, *The Politics of Defense Analysis* (New York: 1974), p. 11 et seq., for a fuller discussion.

2. F. W. Lanchester. *Aircraft in Warfare* (London: 1916).

3. C. P. Snow, *Service and Government* (Cambridge, MA: 1960), chap. 3.

4. C. Webster and N. Frankland, *The Strategic Air Offensive Against Germany, 1939–45*, vol. 3 (London: 1961), pp. 302–303.

5. Lord Zuckerman, *Scientists in War* (London: 1966), pp. 114–15.

6. See Professor Blackett's memorandum on the subject written in 1941 and reproduced in Air Ministry Monograph *The Origins and Development of Operational Research in the RAF* (London: 1963), pp. 189–91.

7. For a fuller description, see J. W. Gibson, "Systems Analysis in British Defence Policymaking," in *The Management of Defence*, ed. L. W. Martin (London: 1976).

8. *Second Report of the House of Commons Defence Committee, Ministry of Defence Organisation and Procurement*, vol. 1, paras. 27 and 136 (viii).

9. RAND Corporation, *26th Anniversary Volume* (Santa Monica, CA: 1973), p. iv.

10. See B. Smith, *The RAND Corporation* (Cambridge, MA: 1966), for a full study of this period.

11. See B. Smith, "Strategic Expertise and National Security Policy," *Public Policy* 13 (1964), for a fuller discussion of this period.

12. R. J. Art, *The TFX Decision: McNamara and the Military* (Boston MA: 1968), pp. 161–162.

13. See C. Murdock, *Defense Policymaking* (Albany, NY: 1974), pp. 76–86, for a fuller discussion of this subject.

14. Ibid., p. 101.

15. Ibid., p. 102.

16. J. Crecine, *Defense Budgeting Constraints and Organisational Adaptation*, Institute of Public Policy Studies Paper No. 6 (Ann Arbor, MI: 1969).

17. L. W. Martin, *Arms and Strategy* (London: 1973), p. 284.

18. M. Armacost, *The Politics of Weapons Innovation: The Thor/Jupiter Controversy* (New York: 1969), passim.

19. *Report of the Secretary of Defense James R. Schlesinger to the Congress on the FY 1975 Budget*, p. 44.

Chapter Eleven

1. Notably, S. Huntington in *The Common Defense* (New York: 1961), chap. 6.

2. See. J. R. Schlesinger, *Defense Planning and Budgeting: The Issue of Centralized Control*, RAND Paper P-3831 (Santa Monica, CA: 1968).

3. It is certainly arguable that congressional opposition had much to do with the failure to provide the fast deployment logistics ships during the period in question, but A. H. Clough's saying "Thou shalt not kill but needst not strive officiously to keep alive" seems applicable here.

4. This statement is based on interviews held in the United States in 1975.

5. J. R. Schlesinger, *Defense Planning and Budgeting: The Issue of Centralized Control.*

6. J. R. Schlesinger, *Department of Defense, Annual Report FY 1975* (Washington, DC: 1974), p. 217.

7. I am indebted to colleagues in the Research Directorate, National Defense University, Washington, DC, in 1982–83, for this information.

8. R. Art, *The TFX Decision* (Boston, MA: 1968), p.166.

9. See University of Southampton collected papers on *Defence Planning and Weapons Technology* (Southampton: 1969), for a fuller discussion.

10. See R. Coulam, *Illusions of Choice* (Princeton, NJ: 1977), for an excellent treatment of the problem of implementing unpopular decisions in this field.

11. The Defense Systems Acquisition Review Committee would also have a part to play in this process, but could not be expected, without outside support, to pass judgment on such a sensitive issue.

12. For a fuller description, see Memorandum DP19 HCDC 145/1 presented by the Ministry of Defence to the House of Commons Defence Committee in vol. 2 of the *Second Report from the Defence Committee 1981–82*, paras. 13–21.

13. M. Howard, *The Central Organisation of Defence* (London: 1970), p. 31.

14. *Second Report from the House of Commons Defence Committee 1981–82*, vol. 1, paras. 27 and 136 (vii).

15. Participatory management also helped to secure the cooperation of the Services in the drastic reduction in defence spending after the Vietnam war.

16. J. R. Fox, *Arming America* (Cambridge, MA: 1974), p. 459.

17. R. Burt, *Defence Budgeting: The British and American Cases* (London: 1975), p. 31.

Chapter Twelve

1. M. Howard, *The Central Organisation of Defence* (London: 1970), pp. 14–15.

2. R. Hastie Smith, "The Tin Wedding," *Seafood House Papers* (London: 1974), p. 36.

3. M. Howard, *The Central Organisation of Defence,* (London: 1970), p. 8 and app. 1.

4. J. C. Ries, *The Management of Defense* (Baltimore, MD: 1964), p. 207.

Chapter Thirteen

1. N. Machiavelli, *The Prince*, Penguin ed. (London: 1961), p. 51.

2. A. Wildavsky, *The Politics of the Budgeting Process*, 3d ed. (Boston, MA: 1979), p. 216.

3. US, Congress, Congressional Budget Office, *Advance Budgeting, A Report to Congress* (Washington, DC: 1977).

4. A. Wildavsky, *The Politics of the Budgeting Process*, p. 263.

5. H. Heclo, *A Government of Strangers* (Washington, DC: 1977), p. 103.

6. See especially H. Heclo, *A Government of Strangers*, chap. 3.

7. The reference is to "Yes Minister," a BBC-TV comedy series published in book form in 1981 by BBC London.

8. An interesting article on this subject is "Thatcher's Mandarins," *Sunday Times*, London, 11 July 1982.

Bibliography

Books and Periodicals

Albion, Robert and Connery, Robert. *Forrestal and the Navy*. New York: Columbia University Press, 1962.

Allison, Graham T. *The Essence of Decision*. Boston, MA: Little, Brown, 1971.

Armacost, Michael, *The Politics of Weapon Innovation*. New York: Columbia University Press, 1969.

Art, Robert J. *The TFX Decision*. Boston, MA: Little Brown, 1968.

Barnard, Chester I. *The Functions of the Executive*. Boston, MA: Harvard University Press, 1938.

Barrett, Archie D. *Reappraising Defense Organization: An Anclysis Based on the Defense Organization Study of 1977–1980*. Washington, DC: National Defense University Press, 1983.

Bartlett, Christopher J. *The Long Retreat*. London: Macmillan, 1972).

Bauer, Raymond and Gergen, Kenneth, eds. *A Theory of Policy Formulation*. New York: Collier-Macmillan, 1968.

Blackett, Patrick. *The Origins and Development of Operational Research in the RAF*. London: H.M. Stationery Office, 1963.

Blau, Peter. *Bureaucracy in Modern Society*. New York: Random House, 1956.

Bobrow, Davis B., ed. *Components of Defense Policy*. Chicago: Rand McNally, 1965.

Brodie, Bernard. *War and Politics*. London: Macmillan, 1974.

Brown, Seyom. *The Faces of Power*. New York: Columbia University Press, 1968.

Brundage, Percival F. *The Bureau of the Budget*. New York: Praeger, 1970.

Burt, Richard. *Defence Budgeting: The British and American Cases.* London: International Institute for Strategic Studies, 1975.

Caraley, Demetrios. *The Politics of Military Unification.* New York: Columbia University Press, 1966.

Clapp, Priscilla and Halperin, Morton, eds. *United States-Japanese Relations in the 1970s.* Cambridge, MA: Harvard University Press, 1974.

Coulam, Robert. *Illusions of Choice: The F111 and the Problem of Weapons Acquisition Reform.* Princeton, NJ: Princeton University Press, 1977.

Crecine, John. *Defense Budgeting: Constraints and Organizational Adaptation.* Institute of Public Policy Studies, Discussion Paper No. 6. Ann Arbor, MI: University of Michigan Press, 1969.

Cyert, Richard M. and March, James G. *A Behavioral Theory of the Firm.* Englewoods Cliffs, NJ: Prentice Hall, 1963.

Enke, Stephen, ed. *Defense Management.* Englewoods Cliffs, NJ: Prentice-Hall, 1967.

Enthoven, Alain and Smith, K. Wayne. *How Much is Enough?* New York: Harper and Row, 1971.

Eisenhower, Dwight D. *Memoirs* vols. 1 and 2. New York: 1963, 1965.

Finer, Samuel E. *Comparative Government.* London: Penguin Books, 1974.

Fox, J. Ronald. *Arming America.* Cambridge, MA: Harvard University Press, 1974.

Gilpin, Robert and Wright, Christopher, eds. *Scientists and National Policymaking.* New York: Columbia University Press, 1964.

Greenwood, David. *Budgeting for Defence.* London: Royal United Services Institute for Defence Studies, 1972.

Halberstam, David. *The Best and the Brightest.* London: Random House, 1972.

———. *The Powers That Be.* New York: Alfred A. Knopf, 1979.

Halperin, Morton. "The President and the Military." *Foreign Affairs* (January 1972).

———. *Bureaucratic Politics and Foreign Policy.* Washington, DC: Brookings Institution, 1974.

Hammond, Paul. *Organizing for Defense.* Princeton, NJ: Princeton University Press, 1961.

Hanrieder, Wolfram, F., ed. *Comparative Foreign Policy.* New York: McKay, 1971.

Hartley, Anthony. *American Foreign Policy in the Nixon Era.* London: International Institute of Strategic Studies, 1975.

Heclo, Hugh and Wildavsky, Aaron. *The Private Government of Public Money.* London: Macmillan, 1973.

Heclo, Hugh. *A Government of Strangers.* Washington, DC: The Brookings Institution, 1977.

Hitch, Charles J. *Decisionmaking for Defense.* Berkeley, CA: University of California Press, 1965.

Hofstadter, Richard. *The American Political Tradition.* New York: Random House, 1957.

Howard, Michael. *The Central Organisation for Defence.* London: Royal United Services Institute for Defence Studies, 1970.

———. "*Civil-Military Relations in Great Britain and USA, 1945–1958.*" *Political Science Quarterly* (March 1960).

Huntington, Samuel. *The Common Defense.* New York: Columbia University Press, 1961.

———. "Strategic Planning and the Political Process." *Foreign Affairs* (1960).

Johnson, Franklyn. *Defence by Committee.* London: Oxford University Press, 1960.

———. *Defence by Ministry.* New York: Holmes & Meier, 1980.

Kaufman, William W. *The McNamara Strategy.* New York: Harper-Row, 1964.

Lanchester, Frederick W. *Aircraft in Warfare.* London: Constable & Co., Ltd., 1916.

Legere, Lawrence. "Defense Spending: A Presidential Perspective." *Foreign Policy* (Spring 1972).

Lindblom, Charles. "The Science of 'Muddling Through'." *Public Administration Review* 19 (1959).

——— *The Intelligence of Democracy*. New York: The Free Press, 1965.

McLean, Joseph E., ed. *The Public Service and University Education*. Princeton, NJ: Princeton University Press, 1949.

Macmillan, Harold. *Tides of Fortune*. London: Macmillan, 1969.

Martin, Laurence W., ed. *The Management of Defence*. London: Macmillan, 1976.

———. "The Market for Strategic Ideas in Britain: The 'Sandys' Era." *American Political Science Review* 56 (March 1962).

Monypenny, William F. and Buckle, George E. *Life of Benjamin Disraeli*, vol. 4, London: John Murray, 1910–20.

Murdock, Clark. *Defense Policy Making*. Albany, NY: State University of New York Press, 1974.

Murray, Douglas J. and Viotti, Paul R. eds. *The Defense Policies of Nations*. Baltimore, MD: Johns Hopkins University Press, 1982.

Neustadt, Richard E. *Alliance Politics*. New York: Columbia University Press, 1970.

Radway, Laurence. *Foreign Policy and National Defence*. Glenview, IL: Scott, Foresman, 1969.

RAND. *25th Anniversary Volume*. Santa Monica, CA: Rand Publications, 1973.

Roherty, James M. *Decisions of Robert S. McNamara*. Coral Gables, FL: University of Miami Press, 1970.

———. ed. *Defense Policy Formation*. Durham, NC: Carolina Academic Press, 1980.

Rosecrance, Richard N. *Defence of the Realm*. New York: Columbia University Press, 1968.

Sanders, Ralph. *Politics of Defence Analysis*. New York: Dunellen, 1973.

Schick, Allen. *Congress and Money*. Washington, DC: The Urban Institute, 1980.

———. "A Death in the Bureaucracy." *Public Administration Review* (March 1973).

Schlesinger, James R. *Defense Planning and Budgeting: The Issue of Centralized Control*. RAND Paper P–3831. Santa Monica, CA: Rand Publications, 1968.

Schultze, Charles L. *The Politics and Economics of Public Spending*. Washington, DC: The Brookings Institution, 1968.

Smith, Bruce. *The RAND Corporation*. Cambridge, MA: Harvard University Press, 1966.

Snow, Charles P. *Science and Government*. Cambridge, MA: Harvard University Press, 1960.

Snyder, William P. *The Politics of British Defense Policy, 1945–1962*. Columbus, OH: Ohio State University Press, 1964.

Steinbruner, John. *The Cybernetic Theory of Decision*. Princeton, NJ: Princeton University Press, 1974.

Stone, I. F. *Polemics and Prophecies 1967–70*. New York: Random House, 1970.

Taylor, Maxwell. *The Uncertain Trumpet*. New York: Harper and Row, 1959.

Truman, Harry S. *Memoirs*, vol. 2. London: Signet Library, 1956.

Waltz, Kenneth. *Foreign Policy and Democratic Politics*. Boston: Little, Brown, 1976.

Webster, Charles and Frankland, Noble. *The Strategic Air Offensive Against Germany* 1939–45, vol. 3. London: 1961.

Wildavsky, Aaron. *The Politics of the Budgetary Process*. 3rd ed. Boston, MA: Little, Brown, 1979.

Williams, Geoffrey and Reed, B. *Denis Healey*. London: 1971.

Zuckerman, Lord (formerly Sir Solly Zuckerman). *Scientists in War*. London: Hamilton-Hamish, 1966.

Government Documents

UNITED KINGDOM

Annual Defence White Papers. London.

Cmd 1431 Defence White Paper. London, 1961.

Cmd 2097 *Central Organisation for Defence*. London, 1963.

Cmd 410 *Scrutiny of Public Expenditure and Administration*. London, 1969.

Cmd 691 *First Report from the Expenditure Committee of the House of Commons* 1975–76. London, 1975.

22-I *Second Report of the Defence Committee of the House of Commons 1981–82. Ministry of Defence Organisation and Procurement*, vols. 1 and 2. London, 1982.

UNITED STATES

Annual Defense Department Reports. Washington, DC.

US. Congress. Joint Economic Committee. Subcommittee on Priorities and Economy in Government. *The Analysis and Evaluation of Public Expenditure. The PPB System*, vol. 3, 91st Cong., 1st sess., Washington, DC, 1969.

US. Congress. Joint Economic Committee. Subcommittee on Economy in Government. *PPBS Progress and Potentials, Hearings.* 90th Cong., 1st sess., September 1976.

US. Congress. Senate. Committee on Government Operations. Subcommittee on National Security and International Operations. *Hearings*, pt. 2. 90th Cong., 1st sess., 1976.

US. Congress. House. Committee on Armed Services. Investigations Subcommittee. *Hearings on Reorganization Proposals for the Joint Chiefs of Staff.* 97th Cong., 2nd sess., 1982.

US. Congress. Congressional Budget Office. *Advance Budgeting: A Report to Congress*, Washington, DC, 1977.

Index

T

V

W

Z